# College Entrance Exams Practice for Science

# Practice Tests for the ACT®

ACT is a registered trademark of ACT, Inc., which was not involved in the production of, and does not endorse, this product.

Printed in the United States of America



ISBN 13: 978-0-55-402160-7
ISBN 10: 0-55-402160-9

1 2 3 4 862 11 10 09 08

# Contents



## Practice Tests for the ACT®



## Practice Test Answer Sheets

# Introduction

This workbook consists of practice activities designed to prepare your students to take the ACT®. The questions in this workbook cover key concepts taught in chapters of *Holt McDougal Chemistry*, *Modern Chemistry*, *Holt McDougal Biology*, *Modern Biology*, *Holt McDougal Earth Science*, and *Holt McDougal Science Spectrum*: *Physical Science*. This breadth of content coverage provides teachers with an opportunity to assess their students' understanding of the essential science knowledge and skills at the high school level. These assessments can help them identify topics or concepts in need of re-teaching or additional practice and should be used to inform curricular decisions on the classroom or school levels.

# ACT Practice Test 1

Name Date

# Practice Test 1

**DIRECTIONS:** There are seven passages in this test. Each passage is followed by several questions. After reading a passage, choose the best answer to each question. Refer to the passages as often as necessary.

## Passage I

DDT (*1,1,1-trichloro-2,2-bis-(p-chlorophenyl) ethane*) is a powerful insecticide. Between 1939 and 1972, people around the world used DDT to control the populations of mosquitoes and other insects. DDT was banned in the United States in 1972, and banned internationally soon after. Two scientists discuss whether or not DDT should remain banned.

*Scientist 1*

DDT should remain banned. Although DDT is extremely effective at killing insects, it has some serious drawbacks. Organisms exposed to small, nonlethal amounts of DDT in the environment retain the chemical for a long time. Every time they are exposed to DDT, they absorb more of the chemical into their system and store it in their fat. DDT is quite soluble in fats and other lipids. In fact, DDT kills by disrupting the lipid membranes that surround and support an organism's cells. But DDT affects more than the organism that ingests it initially. If a consumer eats organisms that have accumulated DDT, the DDT is passed to those consumers. As predators eat the organisms below them in the food chain, the DDT becomes concentrated in the higher-level predators. Humans and other organisms at the top of their food chains risk accumulating very high levels of DDT this way. This concentrating effect is called *biological magnification*, and it causes serious problems. For example, research indicates that concentrated DDT in raptors was responsible for the thinning of their eggshells, threatening the survival of many species. Because of these unintended side effects, DDT is properly considered an environmental hazard and should remain banned.

*Scientist 2*

Using DDT responsibly can save many lives. More than one million people, most of whom are African children, die every year from malaria, a disease caused by a protozoan that is transmitted to people by mosquitoes. Killing mosquitoes with DDT prevents the spread of malaria. Indoor residual spraying (IRS) is one way to use DDT responsibly. For IRS, well-protected and trained individuals spray the interior walls of a home with an insecticide. The insecticide kills mosquitoes that enter the home. The World Health Organization has established strict guidelines for the use of DDT for IRS. DDT administered according to these guidelines poses no threat to human beings. In spite of DDT's effectiveness, the Persistent Organic Pollutants Treaty has as its goal the elimination of all organic pesticides, including DDT. One reason DDT is so popular for insect control is its low cost. DDT is far more affordable than many other pesticides. Eliminating DDT as an option would force poor nations to buy more expensive products in lower volume, serving fewer people. The original ban on DDT was based on effects from its large-scale use in agriculture. In huge doses, the insecticide was an environmental hazard. But in smaller, controlled applications, DDT is an affordable, life-saving tool.

# Practice Test 1 *continued*

**1.** Which of the following phrases best describes the point of difference between the 2 scientists' assertions?

**A.** The hazards of DDT

**B.** The expense of DDT

**C.** The validity of the research that led to the ban of DDT

**D.** The effect of DDT on insects

**2.** According to Scientist 1, biological magnification can occur *primarily* because:

**F.** DDT kills the vectors that transmit pathogens.

**G.** DDT is lethal in high doses.

**H.** DDT does not leave an organism's body once ingested.

**J.** DDT thins the eggshells of reproducing birds.

**3.** According to Scientist 2, DDT can be used safely for IRS applications because:

**A.** DDT is inexpensive.

**B.** DDT would be used in small-scale, controlled applications.

**C.** DDT would be banned by the Persistent Organic Pollutants Treaty.

**D.** DDT would be used in large-scale agricultural applications.

## Practice Test 1 *continued*

4. Which of the following observations would *strengthen* Scientist 2's argument, if true?

   **F.** Rising levels of DDT are detected in residents after IRS.

   **G.** Falling rates of DDT use are noted in nontropical countries.

   **H.** Rising rates of malaria occur in communities that do not use IRS.

   **J.** Falling rates of malaria occur in communities that use IRS.

5. Which of the following would *most likely* satisfy both scientists?

   **A.** Resuming the use of DDT in agricultural applications

   **B.** Banning the use of all pesticides in IRS applications

   **C.** Formulating an inexpensive, biodegradable insecticide

   **D.** Permitting the sale of DDT to homeowners

6. According to Scientist 1, which organisms are most likely to accumulate the highest concentrations of DDT through biological magnification?

   **F.** Algae that absorb DDT

   **G.** Small fish that eat the algae

   **H.** Bigger fish that eat the smaller fish

   **J.** Bears that eat the bigger fish

# Practice Test 1 *continued*

**Passage II**

The big bang theory is the widely accepted explanation for the formation of the universe. According to the theory, about 14 billion years ago, all the matter and energy of the universe was compressed into an extremely small volume. An explosion of this matter and energy in all directions formed our expanding universe.

The big bang theory was first proposed because of observations of the Doppler effect on the light from stars in distant galaxies. The Doppler effect is the apparent shift in the wavelength of light from a star as the star moves toward or away from Earth. Astronomer Edwin Hubble observed that stars in distant galaxies had red shifts, meaning that they were moving away from our galaxy.

He also discovered that these galaxies were moving away at speeds proportional to their distance from us. This evidence seems to support the idea of an expanding universe. Another facet of the big bang theory is that during the big bang, the universe would have been very hot and that as the universe expands, it cools. Cosmic background radiation, low levels of energy that are distributed evenly throughout the universe, is theorized to be energy that remains from the big bang. This radiation has been observed as very cold, matching the predicted cooling of the universe over billions of years.

Name Date

# Practice Test 1 *continued*

FIGURE 1: TEMPERATURE AND TIME AFTER THE BIG BANG

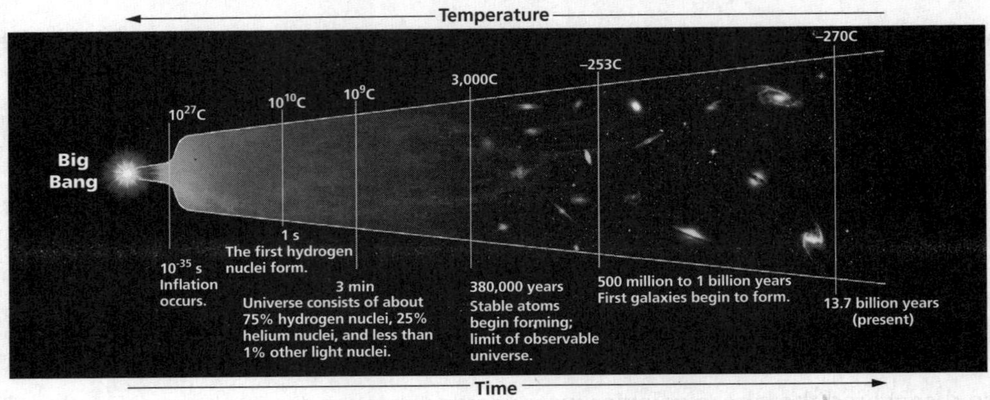


FIGURE 2: RED AND BLUE SHIFT

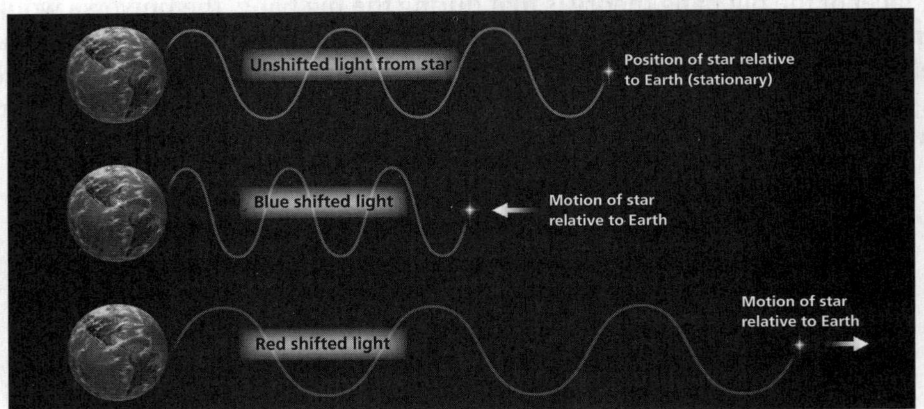


7. The big bang theory says that the universe was once an extremely small, compressed volume of energy and mass. How long after the big bang is it estimated that the first hydrogen nuclei formed?

   **A.** 1 s

   **B.** 3 min

   **C.** 380,000 years

   **D.** 1 billion years

8. Scientists have observed that galaxies are moving away in every direction and that the most distant galaxies are moving away from Earth the fastest. Which of the following explanations for these observations is consistent with the big bang theory?

   **F.** Earth is at the center of the universe.

   **G.** Solar winds push all galaxies away from our solar system.

   **H.** All galaxies formed at the same time several billion years ago.

   **J.** The entire universe has been expanding since the big bang.

# Practice Test 1 *continued*

**9.** The coldest temperature possible, called absolute zero, is about −273°C. The cosmic background radiation is about −270°C. What does this information show to help support the big bang theory?

**A.** The universe has taken billions of years to increase in temperature by 3°C.

**B.** The universe is maintaining a constant temperature as it expands.

**C.** The universe is most likely warming as it expands.

**D.** The universe has been cooling down for billions of years.

**10.** In an expanding universe, observable galaxies are moving away from one another. According to Figure 2, which statement best describes the change in light from stars in most other galaxies due to the Doppler effect?

**F.** The light is not shifted and appears its original color.

**G.** The light is red shifted because the waves are unchanged.

**H.** The light is red shifted as the waves are stretched out.

**J.** The light is blue shifted on Earth, but it is red shifted in other galaxies.

**11.** In addition to the Doppler effect, what assumption is necessary in order to determine the distance from Earth to another galaxy?

**A.** The universe is expanding.

**B.** Similar stars in all galaxies emit light in the same wavelengths.

**C.** Galaxies contain many different types of stars.

**D.** No new galaxies are currently being formed.

**12.** Based on Figure 1, how hot was the universe theorized to be at the moment of the big bang?

**F.** −270°C

**G.** 3,000°C

**H.** 1010°C

**J.** 1027°C

Name Date

# Practice Test 1 *continued*

## Passage III

In 1869, a Russian chemist named Dmitri Mendeleev published the first periodic table of the elements. The table consisted of only 63 known elements. The elements were arranged based on increasing atomic mass, starting with the most abundant and least massive element, hydrogen. An important confirmation of the table occurred as new elements were discovered that fit into gaps that Mendeleev left in the table and whose properties matched those predicted by Mendeleev. Chemists found the periodic table very useful for predicting properties because elements that are in a column share similar properties.

In the current periodic table, elements are arranged based on increasing atomic number, which is the number of protons in an atom of the element. Because each atom has the same number of electrons as protons, the elements are also arranged in order of increasing number of electrons. Electrons are involved in chemical reactions and are responsible for the periodicity of the table. Within the A groups, the number of outer shell electrons, or valence electrons, increases from one to eight from left to right across a period. These are the electrons that are available for chemical reactions with other atoms.

The table now includes elements that do not occur naturally. Atoms that are composed of greater than 92 protons are synthesized using nuclear reactions. These reactions generally occur in particle accelerators in which atoms collide with other atoms or with subatomic particles that are moving at speeds near the speed of light.

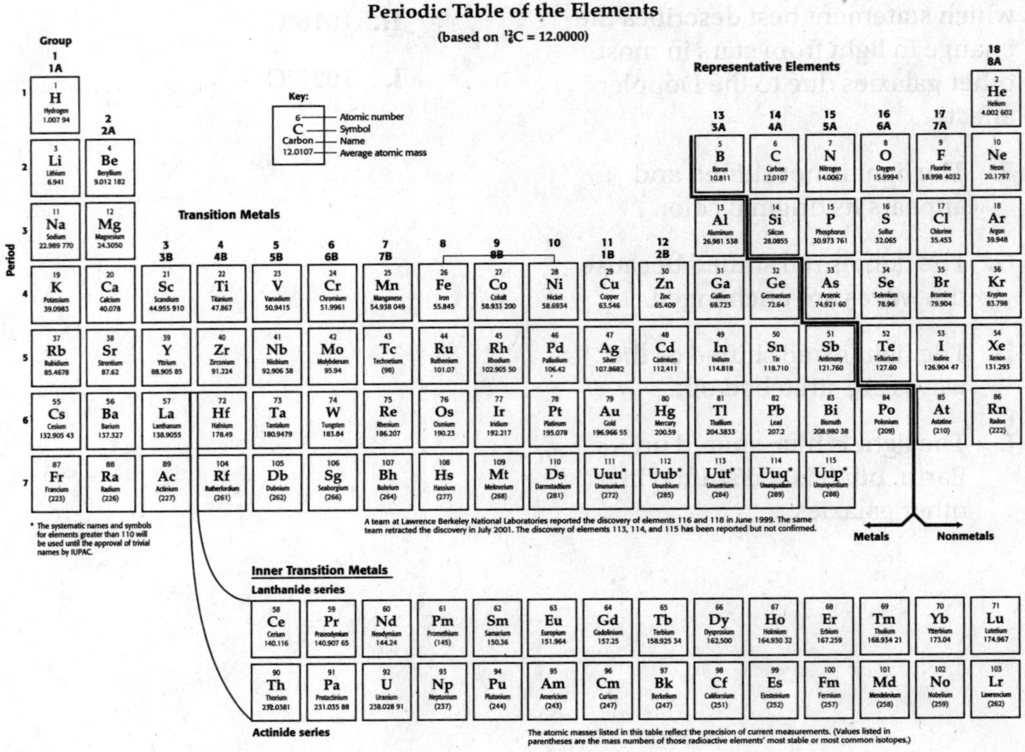

# Practice Test 1 *continued*

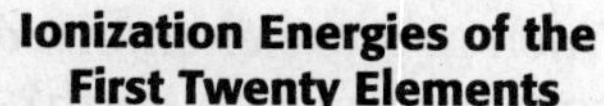


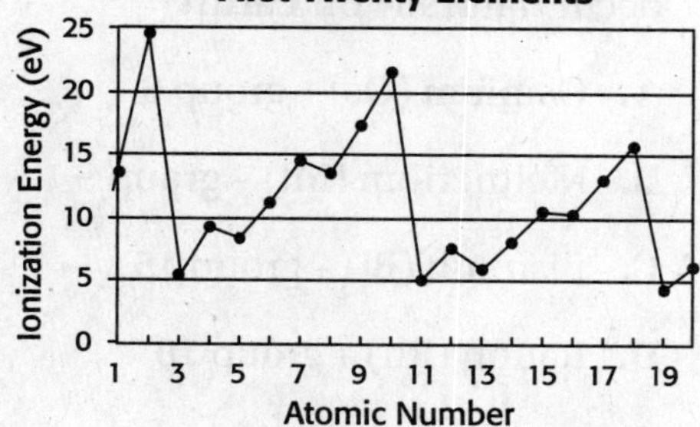


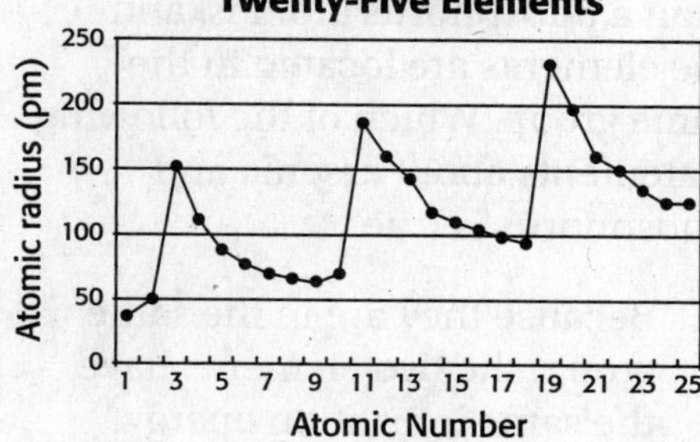


**13.** Based on the information presented, predict the relationship of the atomic radius of an atom of rubidium to the atomic radius of an atom of potassium.

**A.** Because the atomic radii of atoms decrease as you move across a period, the radius of a rubidium atom should be less than that of a potassium atom.

**B.** Because the atomic radii of atoms increase as you move down a column, the radius of a rubidium atom should be greater than that of a potassium atom.

**C.** Because there is no clear trend in the relationship of atomic radii as you move through the periodic table, a prediction cannot be made.

**D.** Because the atomic mass of rubidium is greater than that of potassium, the radius of a rubidium atom is greater than the radius of a potassium atom.

**14.** Bromine, which is located in the same period as calcium, has an atomic number that is greater than calcium's. How does the ionization energy of bromine compare with that of calcium?

**F.** Bromine has the same ionization energy as calcium has because for elements in the same period, an increase in atomic number has no effect on the ionization energy.

**G.** Bromine ionizes more easily than calcium does because when elements are located in the same period, an increase in atomic number corresponds to a decrease in ionization energy.

**H.** Bromine has a higher ionization energy than calcium has because, within a period, ionization energy increases as atomic number increases.

**J.** The relationship cannot be determined from the information provided because the two elements are in different groups on the periodic table.

# Practice Test 1 *continued*

**15.** An arsenic atom is more massive than a phosphorus atom is, and the elements are located in the same group. Which of the following statements about arsenic and phosphorus is true?

**A.** Because they are in the same group, the two elements have the same ionization energy.

**B.** The diameter of an arsenic atom is smaller than the diameter of a phosphorus atom.

**C.** Arsenic and phosphorus have the same number of valence electrons.

**D.** More energy is required to remove an electron from an arsenic atom than to remove an electron from a phosphorus atom.

**16.** Based on the arrangement of elements in the periodic table, what can you predict about the properties of a synthetic element that has an atomic number of 118?

**F.** Element number 118 would be very reactive and have metallic properties.

**G.** Element number 118 would be a nonmetallic element that readily forms salts with metallic elements.

**H.** Element number 118 would be a nonmetallic gas whose atoms are unlikely to react with other atoms.

**J.** Element number 118 would be a metalloid with some properties of both metals and nonmetals.

**17.** Which of these elements does not occur naturally on Earth?

**A.** Osmium (Os) – group 8

**B.** Meitnerium (Mt) – group 9

**C.** Bismuth (Bi) – group 15

**D.** Radon (Rn) – group 18

**18.** Based on its position on the periodic table, which of these atoms has three electrons available to share with or to transfer to other atoms?

**F.** Helium

**G.** Lithium

**H.** Boron

**J.** Oxygen

**19.** An atom of which of these elements has a radius that is greater than the radius of a beryllium atom?

**A.** Carbon

**B.** Aluminum

**C.** Sulfur

**D.** Argon

Name Date

# Practice Test 1 *continued*

**Passage IV**

Weather forecasters are tracking a system of storms west of the Rocky Mountains. They are trying to predict what effect, if any, this approaching weather system will have on the area around St. Louis, MO. Weather forecasters have several tools that they use in an effort to predict the weather. Some of these tools are relatively simple, such as barometers, thermometers, and relative humidity measurements. Other tools are very sophisticated and include weather satellites and Doppler radar that track air masses and computers that use the data collected to make models of possible weather patterns.

The forecasters know that fronts (Figure 1) produce changes in the weather. A cold front is likely to produce storms. When air masses become trapped in an area, pollutants such as ozone can become concentrated in the trapped air, creating a health hazard.

Weather is also influenced by such factors as relative humidity (determined from Figure 2) and barometric pressure (like those in Figure 3).

**Figure 1**

**Figure 2**

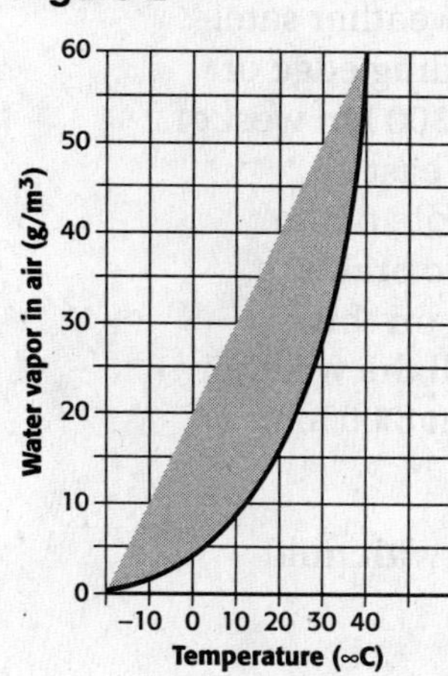


**Figure 3**

| Barometric Pressure Readings | | |
|---|---|---|
| Monday | Tuesday | Wednesday |
| 30.1 | 29.7 | 29.1 |

# Practice Test 1 *continued*

**20.** On the Monday evening news, the forecaster reports that the temperature is 30°C and winds are out of the northwest at 40 km/h. Based on Figure 2, what is the maximum amount of water vapor in the air under these conditions?

**F.** 2 g/m$^3$

**G.** 30 g/m$^3$

**H.** 40 g/m$^3$

**J.** 60 g/m$^3$

**21.** At 6:00 p.m on Wednesday, the forecasters see from weather satellite maps that the leading edge of the cold front is now 300 km west of St. Louis and moving east at 20 km/h. They take note of the changes in barometric pressure since Monday. Based on this information, what will the weather likely be in St. Louis at 8:00 a.m. on Thursday morning?

**A.** Sunny and warm with mild breezes

**B.** Cloudy and overcast

**C.** Windy and rainy with a chance of thunderstorms

**D.** Hot and humid

**22.** While waiting to go on the air, the weather forecaster for the nightly news pops the top on a can of carbonated soda. Gas whooshes out of the can. In what way does the gas model the behavior of air?

**F.** When two air masses that have different pressures meet, air moves from the region of high pressure to the region of low pressure and creates wind.

**G.** The collision of a warm front with a cold front sets off shock waves that result in wind.

**H.** When two air masses that have different pressures meet, the air moves from the region of low pressure to the region of high pressure and creates wind.

**J.** A can of soda is too small of a system to be used as a model for how air behaves.

Name Date

## Practice Test 1 *continued*

**23.** A local radio station in Los Angeles, CA, issues an "ozone alert." Citizens are asked to refrain from such activities as driving unnecessarily and buying gasoline. People with asthma and other lung or breathing disorders are asked to stay indoors. What atmospheric phenomenon could trigger an ozone alert?

**A.** An approaching low pressure air mass

**B.** An electrical disturbance in the ionosphere

**C.** Cirrus clouds moving into the area

**D.** A temperature inversion

**24.** Why do warmer air masses tend to rise above cooler air masses at a front?

**F.** Warmer air masses move faster than cooler air masses move.

**G.** Cooler air masses have less energy and are more dense than warmer air masses.

**H.** Cooler air masses contain more moisture than warmer air masses contain.

**J.** Warmer air masses are affected less by the motion of Earth's surface than cooler air masses are.

**Passage V**

Genetically engineered foods are now on sale in the world's supermarkets, and we do not recognize them because they are not labeled as such. Biotechnologists develop desirable characteristics in an organism by altering its genes or by inserting new genes into the organism's cells. For example, a gene that makes one plant species resistant to pests might be transferred to another plant species. The second plant species would then have the same resistance to pests. Here are two points of view on genetically engineered foods.

*Scientist 1*
Creating genetically engineered food is simply an extension of previous plant breeding techniques. Traditionally, farmers altered the genetic makeup of plants by crossbreeding different strains to combine the best traits of both plants. However, the direct manipulation of genes makes it possible to control genetic changes more precisely and efficiently. These new products are as safe for consumers as plants developed through crossbreeding. Why shouldn't genetically engineered foods sit beside other foods on grocery store shelves? The benefits of creating genetically engineered fruits and vegetables include keeping produce fresh longer, adding nutrients, and creating more-successful crops. For example, by inserting a gene that gives virus resistance to squash plants, scientists could boost the plants' resistance to viral infection. These resistant squash could produce five times the amount of squash per harvest as other squash do. Crops could be developed to grow faster and have higher yields. To combat world hunger, scientists may be able to develop seeds that can grow well in areas that have poor soil or poor water conditions. For more immediate relief, genetically engineered foods that would not spoil as quickly could be shipped to needy nations.

*Scientist 2*
Genetically engineered foods are significantly different from foods developed through traditional methods. Genetic engineering allows genes from any living organism, including genes from animals or bacteria, to be placed into crops. We should be concerned about the safety of foods that contain these "foreign" genes. For example, we should be concerned about the possibility of allergic reactions. Some foods, such as peanuts and shellfish, cause dangerous allergic reactions in many people. If genes from these foods are placed in entirely different products, people who eat these new products and do not know that the new products contain the foreign genes may have allergic reactions. Certain religions have prohibitions against eating pork or other foods. People may object to the insertion of genes from pigs or other prohibited foods into foods they normally eat. Similarly, vegetarians might object to eating foods that contain animal genes. Furthermore, genetically engineered plant species may be accidentally introduced into the wild. Genetic engineering may give a new species an advantage over an existing wild species. If the new species thrives at the expense of the wild species, the wild species could become extinct.

## Practice Test 1 *continued*

**25.** Which of the following points of concern is the most significant difference between the two scientists?

**A.** The volume of food created through genetic engineering

**B.** The safety of genetically engineered food and crops

**C.** The flavors of the food created by genetic engineering

**D.** The expense of genetic research

**26.** According to Scientist 2, people who unknowingly eat modified foods that contain genes from a peanut plant could:

**F.** suffer allergic reactions.

**G.** absorb the genes into their genome.

**H.** have a genetic advantage over other people.

**J.** selectively eliminate the gene while digesting the food.

**27.** Scientist 1 argues that genetic engineering can help solve the problem of:

**A.** overpopulation.

**B.** infectious diseases.

**C.** world hunger.

**D.** air pollution.

Name Date

## Practice Test 1 *continued*

**28.** Which observation, if true, would *weaken* the argument of Scientist 1?

**F.** Genetically engineered squash plants that produce 8 times the amount of squash as normal plants

**G.** Genetically engineered crops that use half as much water as normal plants use

**H.** Genetically engineered crops that have started to grow in a wildlife preserve are out-competing native plants

**J.** Genetically engineered crops that are resistant to pests that kill other plants

**29.** Which observation, if true, would *weaken* the argument of Scientist 2?

**A.** Genetically engineered soybeans have been in widespread use for many years without causing any reactions or environmental problems.

**B.** Researchers determine that food-related allergies kill more than 10,000 people in the United States every year.

**C.** Researchers find that some plants are no longer protected by the biochemicals made by the genes inserted into crops.

**D.** People who practice certain religions cannot eat beef or beef products.

**30.** What part of a cell is changed when a gene is implanted during genetic engineering?

**F.** The proteins that signal genes to switch on and off.

**G.** The DNA that encodes genetic information that controls cell functions.

**H.** The mitochondria that supply the energy for cells to function.

**J.** The connections that allow cells within an organism to communicate with one another.

# Practice Test 1 *continued*

**Passage VI**

The speed of sound is not a constant value. Because the energy of sound waves is carried by a medium, the speed of the waves is affected by the properties of the medium. These properties include the physical state of the medium, the arrangement of particles within the medium, and the energy of the particles.

**Table 1. Speed of Sound in Various Mediums**

| Medium | Speed of sound (m/s) | Medium | Speed of sound (m/s) |
|---|---|---|---|
| **Gases** | | **Liquids at 25°C** | |
| Air (0°C) | 331 | Water | 1490 |
| Air (25°C) | 346 | Sea water | 1530 |
| Air (100°C) | 386 | **Solids at 25°C** | |
| Helium (0°C) | 972 | Copper | 3813 |
| Hydrogen (0°C) | 1290 | Iron | 5000 |
| Oxygen (0°C) | 317 | Rubber | 54 |

**Table 2. Density of Air**

| Temperature | Density ($kg/m^3$) |
|---|---|
| 0 | 1.293 |
| 25 | 1.184 |
| 100 | 0.946 |

A scientist calculated the speed of light in several materials, as listed in Table 3, by using the index of refraction of each material and the value $3.00 \times 10^5$ km/sec as the speed of light in a vacuum.

**Table 3. Speed of Light in Various Mediums**

| Medium | Index of Refraction | Speed of light (km/sec) |
|---|---|---|
| air | 1.003 | 299,000 |
| water | 1.33 | 226,000 |
| sea water | 1.38 | 217,000 |

# Practice Test 1 *continued*

**31.** Which of the following is the best explanation of the effect of temperature on the speed of sound in air?

**A.** The speed of sound increases as the number of particles per unit volume increases.

**B.** The speed of sound increases as the energy of the particles in air increases.

**C.** The speed of sound in air is independent of the temperature.

**D.** The speed of sound in air increases as the volume of air increases.

**32.** A scientist used a sonar device to make a map of the floor of a lake. The device emits a pulse of sound and then measures the time between emitting the pulse and receiving an echo of the sound. At a particular point, this time was measured at 1.5 sec. How deep is the lake at this point, assuming that the water temperature is 25°C?

**F.** 1118 m

**G.** 1490 m

**H.** 2235 m

**J.** 14,900 m

**33.** Based on the data in Table 1, how does the mass of the particles of a gas affect the speed of sound in the gas?

**A.** The speed of sound increases as the mass of a particle of the medium increases.

**B.** The speed of sound increases as the mass of a particle of the medium decreases.

**C.** The speed of sound in a gas is determined by the number of atoms in a molecule of the gas.

**D.** No trend is evident between the speed of sound and the mass of the gas particles.

Name Date

# Practice Test 1 *continued*

**34.** Compare the speed of light with the speed of sound in air, in water, and in sea water. Which hypothesis below could explain the difference in how a change in medium affects the speeds of light and of sound?

**F.** Sound waves have longer wavelengths than light waves have so the nature of the medium affects the speed of sound less than it affects the speed of light.

**G.** Light waves do not require a medium so they always travel at the same speed, but the speed of sound waves is affected by the particles of the medium.

**H.** A denser medium interferes with light waves and causes them to slow down, but a denser medium transmits sound waves more effectively.

**J.** Light waves are mechanical waves so they are not affected by the medium as greatly as sound waves are.

**35.** As a thunderstorm approaches, you observe that you see the flash of the lightning before you hear the sound of the thunder. After a particular flash of lightning, you measure the time between the flash and the sound. If the sound arrives 8 sec after the light, about how far away was the lightning?

**A.** 1.4 km

**B.** 2.8 km

**C.** 4.2 km

**D.** 8.0 km

# Practice Test 1 *continued*

## Passage VII

A group of students performed an experiment in science class using a toy car. A strip of paper tape was attached to the car, and the paper tape was passed through a recording timer. As the car moved, it pulled the paper tape through the timer. The recording timer made dots on the paper tape at regular time intervals. Measuring the distance between dots provided data that could be used to determine the speed of the car.

*Experiment 1*
The car was pushed across a flat surface and then released. The students made the graphs below from the collected data to illustrate the motion of the car after it was released.

**Figure 1**

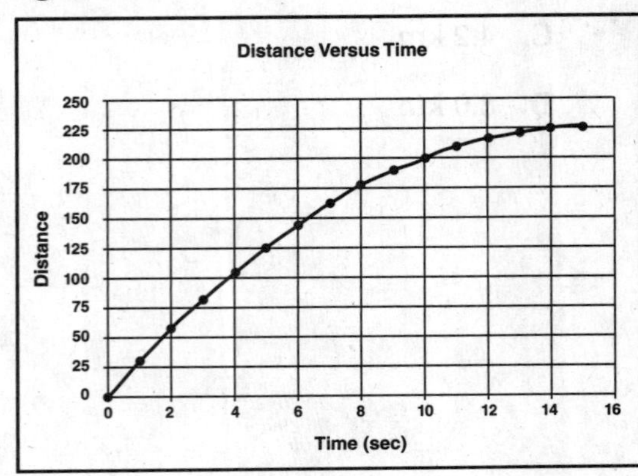


**Figure 2**

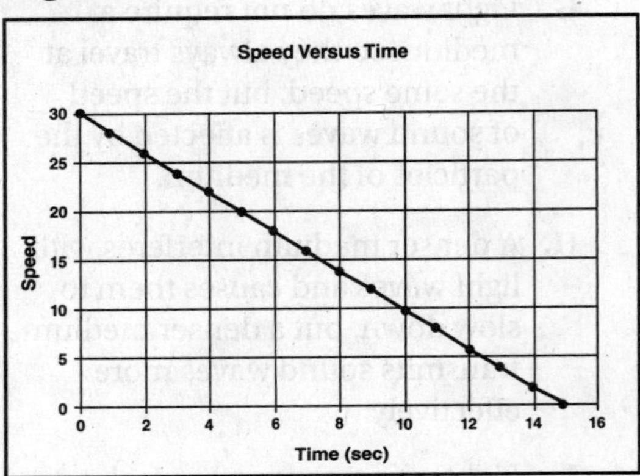


*Experiment 2*
The car was placed at the top of an incline and released. The students did not apply a force to the car to begin its motion. After reaching the bottom of the ramp, the car moved along a flat surface until it came to a complete stop.

*Experiment 3*
A block of wood was placed at the bottom of the ramp. When the car reached the block of wood, it collided with the block and came to an abrupt stop.

## Practice Test 1 *continued*

**36.** In Experiment 1, what was the acceleration of the car after the end of the initial push that started its motion?

**F.** 2 cm/sec

**G.** $-2$ cm/sec$^2$

**H.** $-20$ cm/sec$^2$

**J.** 2 cm/sec$^2$

**37.** The students made Graph 1 and Graph 2 from the data collected during Experiment 2 using the same axes used for Figure 1 and Figure 2 for Experiment 1. Which of the following statements is the best prediction for the general appearance of the graphs for the time during which the car was on the ramp?

**A.** The graphs for Experiment 2 appear very similar to the figures from Experiment 1.

**B.** Graph 1 for Experiment 2 will be similar to Figure 1 for Experiment 1, but Graph 2 will have a positive slope.

**C.** Graph 1 for Experiment 2 will start at (0, 0) and curve upward, and Graph 2 will be a line that has a positive slope.

**D.** The graphs for Experiment 2 will be straight lines, and each line will have a positive slope.

**38.** What contributes to the net force that causes the acceleration shown in Figure 2 for Experiment 1?

**F.** The initial push on the car and gravity

**G.** Gravity and friction

**H.** Friction only

**J.** The initial push on the car and friction

# Practice Test 1 *continued*

**39.** The students repeated Experiment 2, but added a lead weight to the toy car which doubled the car's mass. How would the addition of the weight affect the acceleration of the car on the ramp?

**A.** The acceleration of the heavier car would be half the acceleration of the lighter car.

**B.** The acceleration of the heavier car would be twice the acceleration of the lighter car.

**C.** The acceleration of the heavier car would be twice the acceleration of the lighter car.

**D.** There is not enough information to predict the effect of the weight on the acceleration of the car.

**40.** In Experiment 3, the velocity of the car abruptly changes at the bottom of the ramp. What can be concluded about the acceleration of the car at this instant?

**F.** The instantaneous acceleration of the car is equal to zero because the velocity is reduced to zero.

**G.** The instantaneous acceleration is negative because there is a negative change in velocity.

**H.** The instantaneous acceleration is positive because there is a negative change in velocity.

**J.** The instantaneous acceleration is equal to the negative value of the acceleration due to gravity because the car is slowing down.

# ACT Practice Test 2

# Practice Test 2

## Passage I

The solubility of materials in water varies greatly. For a particular material, solubility varies with the temperature of the solution. Even closely related compounds can have very different solubilities. Some metal salts dissolve in large amounts in water while others are almost insoluble. The solubility of any substance in water depends on the strength of the forces acting between particles of the solute and the strength of the forces acting between the solute particles and water molecules. So, in a highly soluble substance, the net force between solute particles is weaker than the net force between the water molecules and the solute particles.

Graph A shows the results of an experiment in which saturated solutions were made using the maximum amount of metal salts that would dissolve in 100 g of water at different temperatures. Graph B records the solubility of three different gases in water at temperatures ranging from 0°C to 100°C at a constant pressure. In addition to temperature, the solubility of a gas in water depends on pressure. At a given temperature, increasing pressure increases the solubility of a gas.

**SOLUBILITY IN WATER VS. TEMPERATURE FOR VARIOUS MATERIALS**

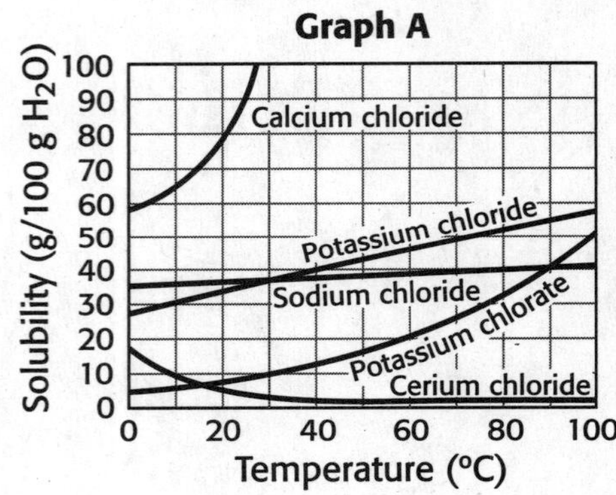


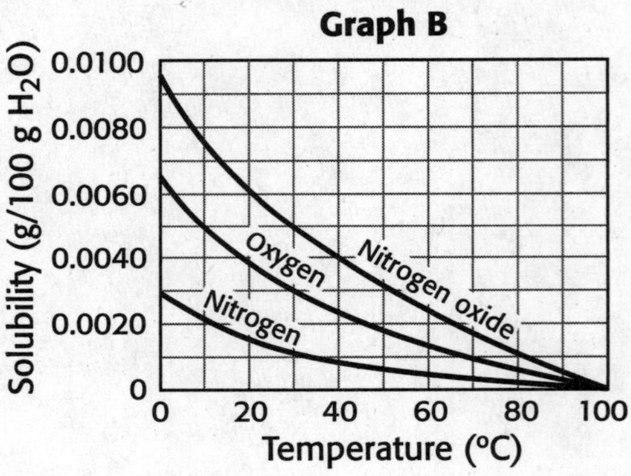


| Temperature (°C) | Solubility of $AgNO_3$ in (g $AgNO_3$/100 g $H_2O$) |
|---|---|
| 0 | 122 |
| 20 | 216 |
| 40 | 311 |
| 60 | 440 |
| 80 | 585 |

| Substance | Formula | Solubility at 20° C (g/100 g H2O) |
|---|---|---|
| Calcium chloride | $CaCl_2$ | 75 |
| Calcium fluoride | $CaF_2$ | 0.0015 |
| Calcium sulfate | $CaSO_4$ | 0.32 |
| Iron(II) sulfide | FeS | 0.0006 |
| Silver chloride | AgCl | 0.00019 |
| Silver nitrate | $AgNO_3$ | 216 |
| Sodium chloride | NaCl | 35.9 |
| Sodium fluoride | NaF | 4.06 |
| Sodium iodide | NaI | 178 |
| Sodium sulfide | $Na_2S$ | 26.3 |

Name Date

# Practice Test 2 *continued*

**1.** Which hypothesis is supported by the data in Graph A and in Table 2?

**A.** The solubility of salts increases as the temperature of the solution increases.

**B.** The solubility of a salt depends on the number of ions in the salt's formula.

**C.** There is no correlation between solvent temperature and solubility for any solute.

**D.** The solubility of salts generally increases as the solution temperature increases.

**2.** Which hypothesis is supported by the data plotted in Graph A and in Graph B?

**F.** The solubilities of gases and of metal salts have the same response to temperature.

**G.** The solubility of nitrogen oxide is the sum of the solubility of nitrogen and the solubility of oxygen.

**H.** The solubility of gases generally decreases as solution temperature increases.

**J.** In general, gases have a greater solubility in water than salts have.

**3.** Which of these statements is correct based on the data presented in Graph A and in Table 1?

**A.** Silver nitrate is less soluble than potassium chloride is at low temperatures but more soluble than potassium chloride is at high temperatures.

**B.** The solubility of silver nitrate is greater than the solubility of calcium chloride at temperatures ranging from 0°C to 100°C.

**C.** The trend in the solubility of silver nitrate is similar to the trend in the solubility of cerium chloride.

**D.** Silver nitrateCalcium chloride is less soluble in water than silver nitrate is at temperatures ranging from 0°C to 28°C.

**4.** Based on Table 2, what is the concentration of a saturated solution of iron(II) sulfide at 20°C?

**F.** 0.006 ppm

**G.** 0.6 ppm

**H.** 6 ppm

**J.** 600 ppm

# Practice Test 2 *continued*

**5.** What can be inferred about the polarity of the gas molecules in Graph B?

**A.** They are polar molecules because only polar materials dissolve in water.

**B.** The polarity of the gas molecules decreases as their temperature increases.

**C.** There is not enough information in the graph to infer anything about the polarity of the gas molecules.

**D.** The molecules are nonpolar because they do not form concentrated solutions in water.

**6.** Based on all of the information provided, which list below correctly orders the materials from least soluble to most soluble in water at 20°C?

**A.** Oxygen, silver chloride, potassium chloride, silver nitrate

**B.** Silver chloride, oxygen, potassium chloride, silver nitrate

**C.** Silver nitrate, potassium chloride, oxygen, silver chloride

**D.** Potassium chloride, oxygen, silver nitrate, silver chloride

**7.** If you look at an unopened bottle of warm soda, there are no bubbles in the liquid. However, when you open the bottle and pour some soda in a glass, bubbles form throughout the solution. Which of these statements best explains the formation of the bubbles?

**F.** The pressure on the soda decreases, the solubility of gas that is dissolved in the soda decreases, and the gas forms bubbles as it comes out of solution.

**G.** When the soda is exposed to nitrogen gas and oxygen gas in the air, these gases bubble into the soda and dissolve.

**H.** The temperature of the soda increases as the soda is poured, so the solubility of the dissolved gases decreases and the gases come out of solution and form bubbles.

**J.** The decrease in pressure causes some of the liquid water to become a vapor and form bubbles of water vapor throughout the soda.

# Practice Test 2 *continued*

**Passage II**

| Rock | Type | Description |
|---|---|---|
| granite | intrusive igneous rock | coarse-grained texture |
| obsidian | extrusive igneous rock | black, shiny surface |
| conglomerate | sedimentary rock | composed of rounded fragments of weathered rock |
| limestone | sedimentary rock | made up of fossilized sea creatures |
| slate | metamorphic rock | hard rock that can be split very easily along planes in the rock |

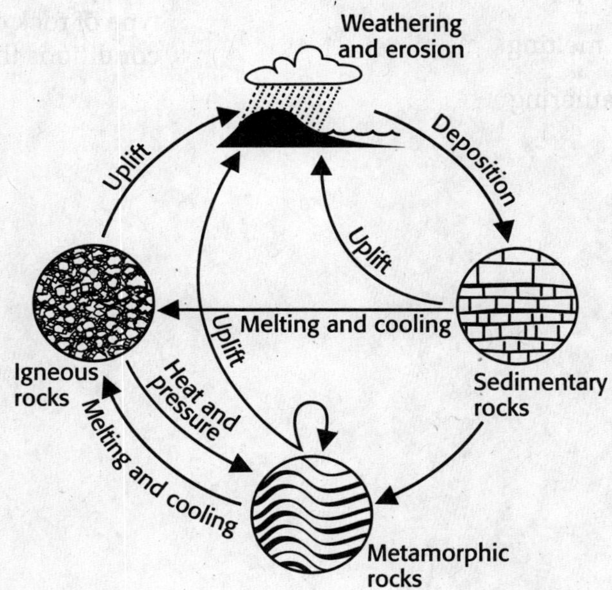

# Practice Test 2 *continued*

8. Examine the rock illustrated below. Based on the features of the rock and the information provided, what are the most recent processes of the rock cycle that occurred in its history?

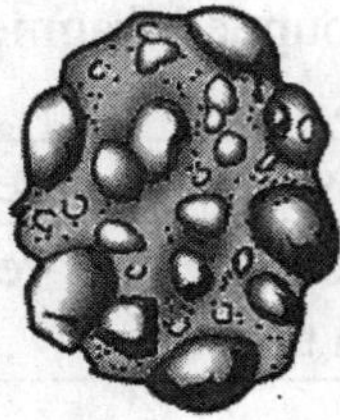

**F.** Melting and uplift

**G.** Erosion and deposition

**H.** Pressure and melting

**J.** Heat and weathering

9. Which statement **best** summarizes the rock cycle?

**A.** Rocks deep below the ground rise to the surface, move back underground, then rise to the surface again.

**B.** Igneous rocks and sedimentary rocks change to metamorphic rocks.

**C.** Each type of rock forms from one other type of rock in a set sequence.

**D.** Rock can change into a different type of rock depending on the conditions that affect it.

# Practice Test 2 *continued*

**10.** In an expanding universe, observable galaxies are moving away from one another. According to Figure 2, which statement best describes the change in light from stars in most other galaxies due to the Doppler effect?

Syenite

Granite

Obsidian

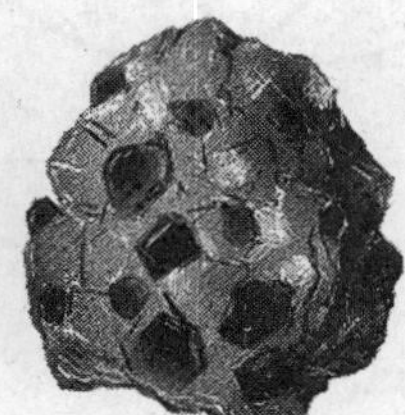

Pegmatite

**F.** Syenite

**G.** Granite

**H.** Obsidian

**J.** Pegmatite

**11.** While exploring a quarry, you find a rock that contains a fossilized imprint of a leaf. Based on the processes that occur during the rock cycle, what do you know about the rock?

**A.** The rock is a sedimentary rock.

**B.** The rock is an igneous rock.

**C.** The rock could be either a sedimentary rock or an igneous rock.

**D.** The rock could be any type of rock because sedimentary rocks become igneous and metamorphic rocks.

**12.** Most of the rock in Earth's crust was formed from the partial melting of materials from the mantle or the crust as a result of tectonic processes. Based on this information and what you know about the rock cycle, how can most of the rock of the crust be classified?

**F.** Mostly sedimentary or metamorphic rock

**G.** Mostly metamorphic or igneous rock

**H.** Mostly sedimentary or igneous rock

**J.** Approximately equal amounts of sedimentary, metamorphic, and igneous rock

## Practice Test 2 *continued*

### Passage III

In predation, an individual of one species, called the *predator*, eats all or part of an individual of another species, called the *prey*. Predation is a powerful force in a community. The relationship between predator and prey influences the size of each population and affects where and how each species lives. Examples of predators include *carnivores*—predators that eat animals—and *herbivores*—predators that eat plants. The graph below shows the general relationship between predators and prey.

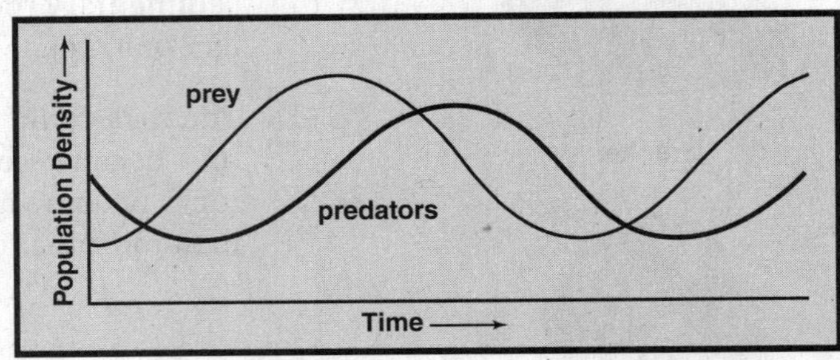


**Figure 1**

For the first study, scientists monitored the populations of moose and wolves on Isle Royale, an island off the coast of Michigan. Data were collected from the late 1950s until the late 1990s.

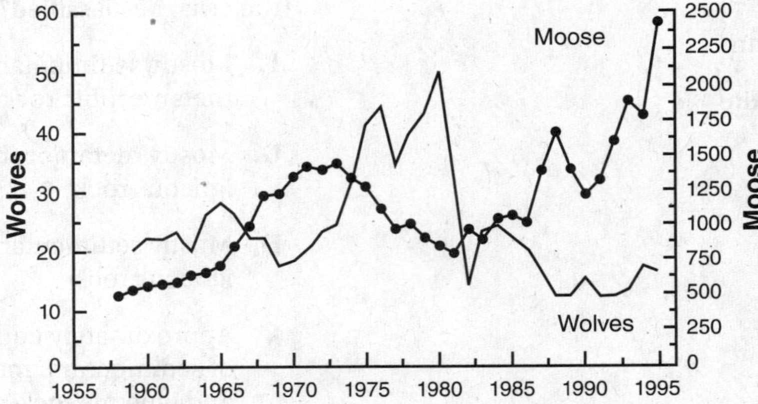


**Figure 2**

# Practice Test 2 *continued*

This set of data was collected by fur trappers in Northern Canada, where the Canada lynx depends on the snowshoe hare for food.

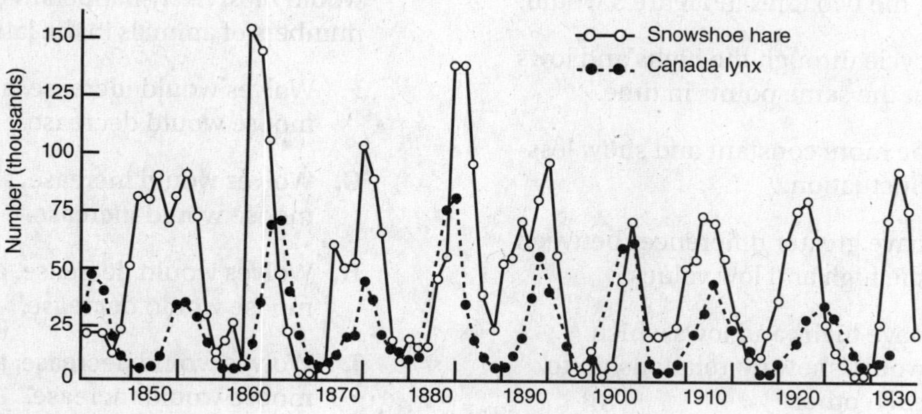


**Figure 3**

**13.** According to Figure 1, the population of predators peaks:

**A.** at the same time as the population of prey peaks.

**B.** shortly before the population of prey peaks.

**C.** after the time at which the population of prey peaks.

**D.** shortly after the population of prey reaches a low.

**14.** According to Figure 2, the number of prey:

**F.** increases ahead of an increase in the number of predators.

**G.** decreases throughout an increase in the number of predators.

**H.** is never greater than the number of predators.

**J.** remains constant during any change in the number of predators.

**15.** Why is it significant that the data in Figure 2 were collected on an island?

**A.** Islands increase predatory behavior toward the captive prey.

**B.** Islands offer prey many places to hide and a consistent food source.

**C.** Islands are seldom inhabited by more than two species, so competition for resources is kept to a minimum.

**D.** Islands help to prevent animals from entering or leaving the populations except through births and deaths.

## Practice Test 2 *continued*

**16.** If the snowshoe hare were not the predominant prey of the Canada lynx, the two lines in Figure 3 would:

**F.** cycle through the highs and lows at the same points in time.

**G.** be more constant and show less fluctuation.

**H.** have greater differences between the high and low values.

**J.** have highs and lows which would show no relationship to each other.

**17.** According to Figure 2, when the lines cross in 1974:

**A.** the moose population was increasing, and the wolf population was decreasing.

**B.** the wolf population was increasing, and the moose population was decreasing.

**C.** both populations were increasing.

**D.** the populations of moose and of wolves were the same.

**18.** According to the pattern in Figure 2, under normal conditions, what would *most likely* happen to the numbers of animals in the late 1990s?

**F.** Wolves would increase, and moose would decrease.

**G.** Wolves would increase, and moose would increase.

**H.** Wolves would decrease, and moose would decrease.

**J.** Wolves would decrease, and moose would increase.

**19.** Suppose that, in 1995, five wolves were removed from the population. If all other conditions remained favorable for the moose, what would *most likely* happen to the moose population in the late 1990s?

**A.** The moose population would decrease.

**B.** The moose population would increase.

**C.** The moose population would stay the same.

**D.** The moose population would decrease, and then increase sharply.

Name Date

# Practice Test 2 *continued*

**Passage IV**

A heating curve shows the changes that a substance undergoes when heat is added to the substance. Any change in temperature and any change in state, or phase change, involves a change in energy. Because temperature is a measure of the average kinetic energy of the particles of a substance, temperature increases as the particles move faster. In fact, temperature in the Kelvin scale is directly proportional to the average kinetic energy of the particles. A temperature in degrees Celsius can be converted to its equivalent temperature in kelvins by adding 273. However, a phase change does not occur with a change in temperature. The energy absorbed during a phase change helps the particles overcome some of the attractions between them and increases their freedom of motion. But because the average kinetic energy of the particles does not change, there is no change in temperature during a phase change.

Figure 1 below shows the results of an experiment by a group of students in a science lab. Heat was added at a steady rate to ice in a beaker, and the temperature was recorded using a thermometer. Energy was added to the sample until it became steam.

**Figure 1**

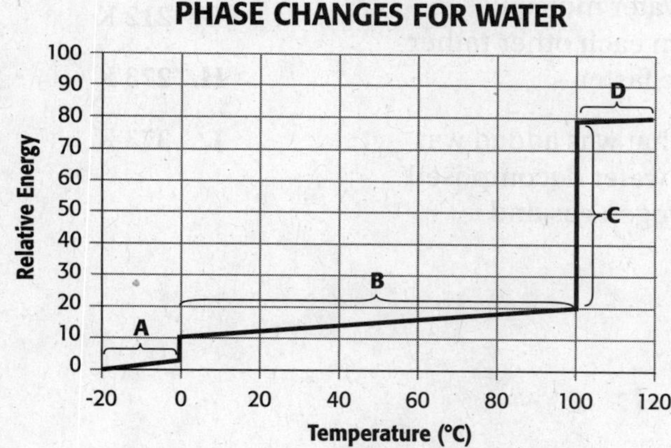


**Figure 2**

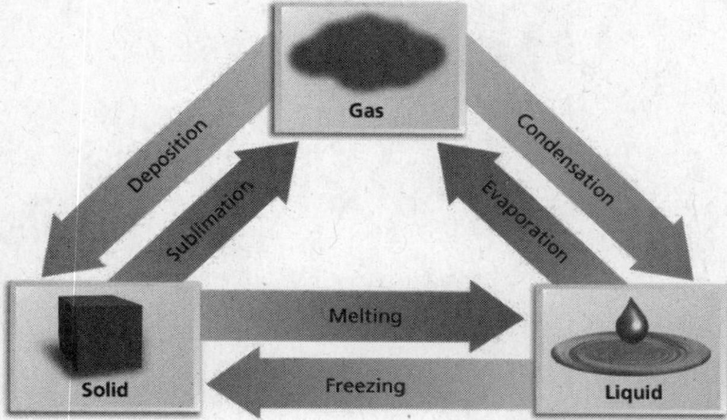

**20.** Students in the lab group made four different hypotheses for the observation that the temperature remained constant for a long time during the section labeled C on the graph. Which is the best explanation for their observation?

**F.** The thermometer was broken, so the temperature reading is not reliable.

**G.** Water in the beaker could not absorb any additional energy, so energy transfer stopped until the water turned to steam.

**H.** All of the energy that was absorbed during this time helped the water molecules to separate from each other rather than to move faster.

**J.** The energy that was added was absorbed as water decomposed to form hydrogen gas and oxygen gas.

**21.** Which section of the graph in Figure 1 represents the period when only liquid water is present in the beaker?

**A.** A

**B.** B

**C.** C

**D.** D

**22.** What is the temperature expressed in kelvins during the section labeled C on the graph?

**F.** 100 K

**G.** 212 K

**H.** 273 K

**J.** 373 K

# Practice Test 2 *continued*

**23.** According to Figure 2, what process occurs as you move from section A to section B in Figure 1?

**A.** Sublimation

**B.** Melting

**C.** Evaporation

**D.** Freezing

**24.** The students repeated the experiment using a different solid. As heat was added, the material became warmer. Eventually, the temperature stopped rising and the solid material began to disappear, but no liquid formed. What explanation should they propose as a hypothesis to explain their observation when they write the lab report?

**F.** A chemical reaction with oxygen in the air converted the material to carbon dioxide and water vapor.

**G.** The process of sublimation occurred as the material changed directly from solid to gas as heat was added.

**H.** The material melted, but because it is liquid only in a very narrow temperature range, it evaporated immediately.

**J.** There was an error in the experimental design that prevented the solid from melting as heat was added.

## Passage V

A scientist planted 800 seeds in containers of damp soil. Half the seeds were placed in direct sunlight. The other 400 seeds were kept in total darkness. All other conditions were the same for both groups. After seven days, all 800 seeds had sprouted and had produced leaves. The plants from the 400 seeds that were kept in total darkness had white leaves. Green leaves developed on 296 of the plants grown in sunlight, and white leaves developed on 104 of the plants grown in sunlight. All 800 plants were then placed in sunlight for two weeks. After 14 days in sunlight, the leaves of 305 of the 400 plants that had originally been kept in darkness had turned green. The other 95 plants in this group remained white.

**Figure 1**

**SEED SPROUTING EXPERIMENT**

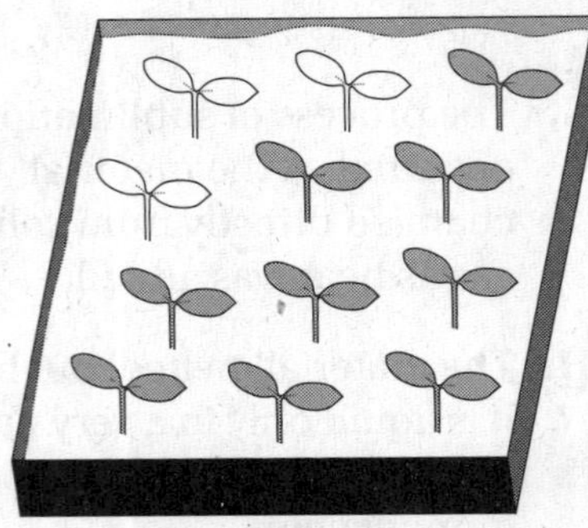

Seeds sprouted in sunlight
**Group A**

Seeds sprouted in darkness
**Group B**

**Figure 2**

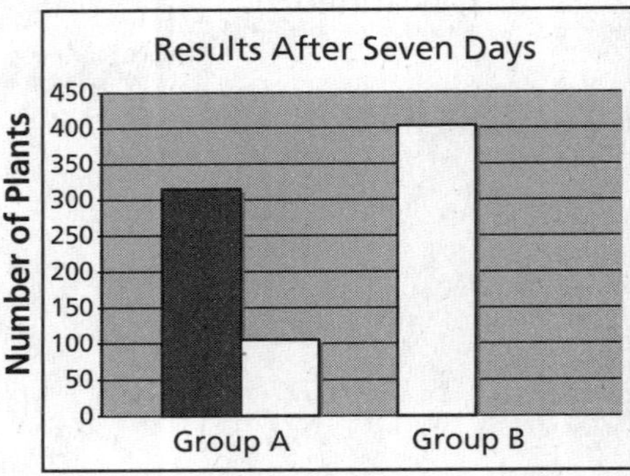


**Figure 3**

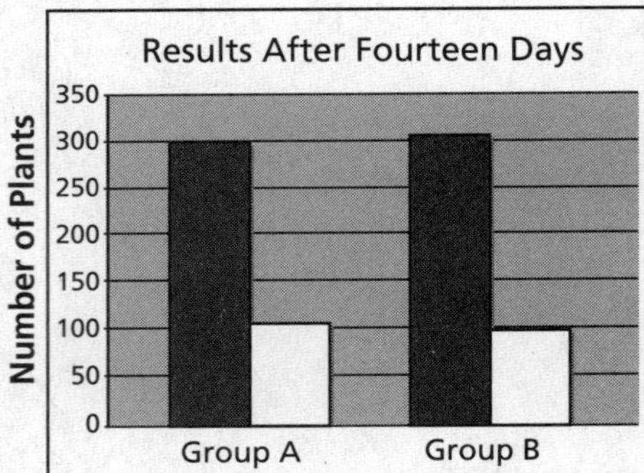


**Key:** ■ = Green Leaves
□ = White Leaves

Name Date

# Practice Test 2 *continued*

**25.** Based on Figure 2 and Figure 3, what percent of the plants remained white even after they had been exposed to sunlight?

**A.** 76%

**B.** 35%

**C.** 25%

**D.** 10%

**26.** What was the dependent variable in this experiment?

**F.** Amount of light

**G.** Leaf color

**H.** Number of seeds

**J.** Duration of the experiment

**27.** What is the best explanation for the observations in the experiment described above?

**A.** Green leaf color is not an inherited characteristic in these plants.

**B.** The presence or absence of light does not affect the development of green leaf color.

**C.** The color of these plants depends on both the environmental conditions and the genetic makeup of the plant.

**D.** The white leaf color is a dominant trait because some plants remained white even when placed in lighted conditions.

**28.** In Passage V, the statement, "All other conditions were the same for both groups" is included in order to:

**F.** eliminate any sources of multiple explanations of the outcome of the experiment that did not relate to the light differences.

**G.** show that the experimental design did not use controls.

**H.** indicate that the scientist doing the experiment did not think of all possible alternative conditions that could have been tested.

**J.** show that this experiment was designed to simulate real-world conditions.

**29.** Why did exposing the plants to sunlight for a second time, as recorded in Figure 3, contribute important data to this experiment?

**A.** It shows that plants are flexible organisms.

**B.** It shows that genes do not play a role in leaf color.

**C.** It shows that the ratio of green-leaved plants to white-leaved plants was dependent on the environmental conditions during sprouting.

**D.** It shows that the outward appearance of the plants was dependent on the genes of the plants and not just on the environmental conditions.

**30.** What can you conclude from these experimental results?

**F.** Plants will develop green leaves after exposure to sunlight.

**G.** When exposed to sunlight, 3 out of 4 plants develop green leaves regardless of initial sprouting conditions.

**H.** Throughout their lives, more plants sprouted in sunlight have green leaves than plants sprouted in darkness have.

**J.** Plants sprouted in darkness suffer genetic defects that affect leaf color.

Name Date

# Practice Test 2 *continued*

**Passage VI**

Climate scientists use evidence from the past to predict future trends in climate. Although everyday experience would make climate seem like a fairly constant thing, evidence of changes over thousands to millions of years shows that climate is volatile and can change drastically. Because human activities are causing changes in the level of carbon dioxide in the atmosphere, scientists are studying the relationship between carbon dioxide and world climates.

The theory that explains the correlation of carbon dioxide and climate is the greenhouse effect. As the level of carbon dioxide increases, the atmosphere absorbs and reflects more of the energy that radiates from Earth's surface and the temperature of the atmosphere increases.

**Figure 1 CHANGES IN CARBON DIOXIDE AND TEMPERATURE IN THE LAST 400,000 YEARS**

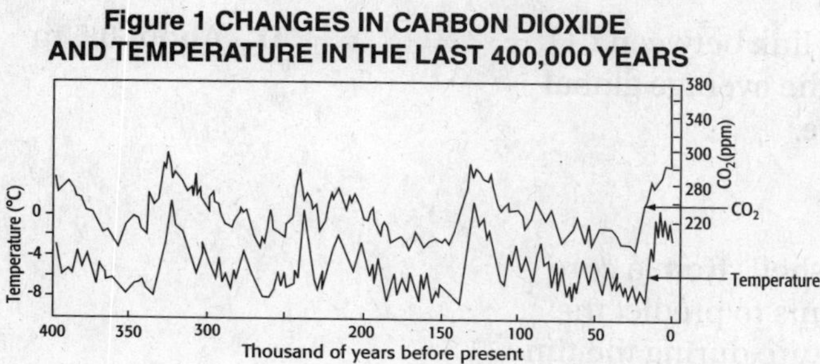


**Figure 2 METHODS OF STUDYING PAST CLIMATES**

| Method | What is measured | What is indicated | Length of time measured |
|---|---|---|---|
| Ice cores | concentrations of gases in ice and meltwater | High levels of $CO_2$ indicate warmer climate; ice ages follow decreases in $CO_2$. | hundreds of thousands of years |
| Sea-floor sediment | concentration of $^{18}O$ in shells of microorganisms | High $^{18}O$ levels indicate cool water; lower $^{18}O$ levels indicate warm water | hundreds of thousands of years |
| Fossils | pollen types, leaf shapes, and animal body adaptations | Flower pollens and broad leaves indicate warm climates; evergreen pollens and small, waxy leaves indicate cool clmates; animal fossils show adaptations to climate changes | millions of years |
| Tree rings | ring width | Thin rings indicate cool weather and less precipitation | hundreds to thousands of years |

**Figure 3 PREDICTED SEA-LEVEL CHANGES**

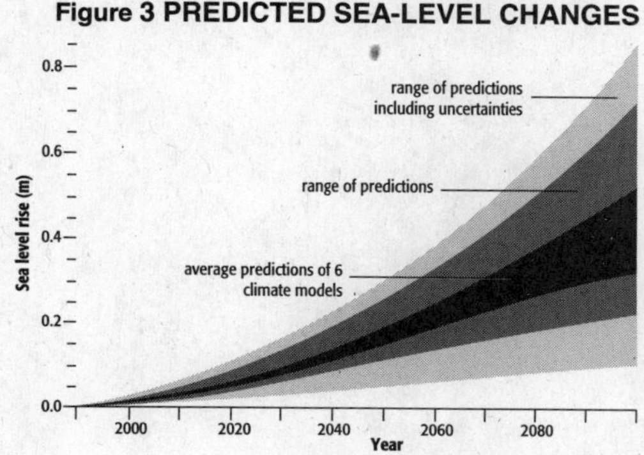

**31.** According to the historical record, as levels of $CO_2$ in the atmosphere increase, what happens to the average global temperature?

**A.** The average global temperature increases.

**B.** The average global temperature decreases.

**C.** The average global temperature stays the same.

**D.** There is no link between $CO_2$ levels and the average global temperature.

**32.** A scientist has shells from a core sample and wants to predict the ocean temperature during the time period when the shells formed. What would the scientist measure?

**F.** Concentration of $CO_2$ in the shells

**G.** Amount of rings in the shells

**H.** Types of pollen in the shells

**J.** Concentrations of oxygen isotopes in the shells

**33.** When scientists make predictions, they include in their report a measure of the uncertainty associated with their predictions. Based on Figure 3, what is the **least** amount that the sea level should rise by the year 2100?

**A.** About 0.1 m

**B.** About 0.2 m

**C.** About 0.3 m

**D.** About 0.5 m

**34.** Why are scientific predictions concerning climate change important to society at large?

**F.** Predictions can tell us which areas of the world will be unaffected by climate change and help us plan the migration of large populations.

**G.** People can find out the history of the Earth's climate changes to better understand what is occurring in the present.

**H.** People can plan for changes in the climate that are predicted to occur thousands of years from now.

**J.** Society can change its activities to minimize the negative effects these activities have on humans and on the environment.

**35.** What would be the most likely explanation for the straight, almost vertical line in the graph of $CO_2$ during recent times when the graph appears as a fluctuating jagged line throughout most of Figure 2?

**A.** Human activity has resulted in an increase in carbon dioxide production from multiple sources in recent times.

**B.** Large amounts of carbon dioxide are being released from melting glaciers.

**C.** Large decreases in the populations of shell-forming animals have resulted in a reduced uptake of carbon dioxide from the atmosphere.

**D.** Ocean levels are rising, which results in an increase in the number of aquatic plants that produce carbon dioxide.

**Passage VII**

During an experiment to study the force of gravity, a scientist measured the rate at which a feather and a rock fall, as illustrated below. The observed rate was the same for both objects, even though they have very different masses.

**Figure 1**
**VELOCITIES OF FALLING OBJECTS**

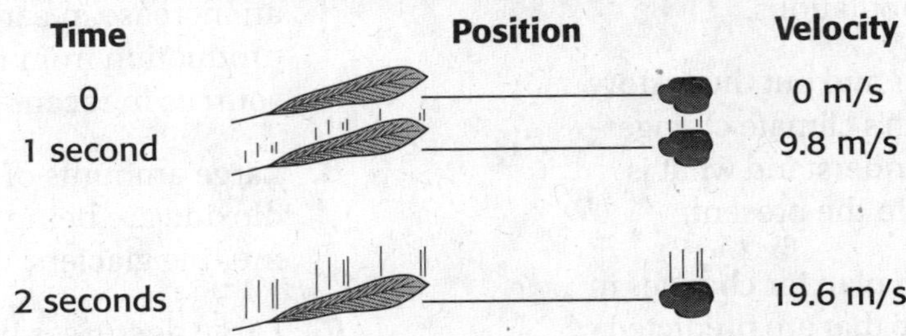


A group of students decided to reproduce the experiment by dropping a rock and a feather from a third floor window of the school into the courtyard below. They recorded the following data.

**Table 1**

| Gravity Experiment | | |
|---|---|---|
| **Trial** | **Time for rock to fall (s)** | **Time for feather to fall (s)** |
| 1 | 1.2 | 5.8 |
| 2 | 1.2 | 6.3 |
| 3 | 1.2 | 6.4 |

**36.** Which of the following hypotheses could be a correct explanation for the difference in the results of the two experiments?

**F.** The scientist was using a feather that had more mass than the rock had, but the students were using a feather that had less mass than the rock had.

**G.** The students performed their experiment outdoors but the scientist was in a laboratory, so the gravitational accelerations were different.

**H.** The scientist performed the experiment in a vacuum but the students did not, so different forces affected the objects.

**J.** The scientist dropped the feather in a vertical orientation, but the students dropped the feather in a horizontal orientation.

**37.** Based on Figure 1, what is the acceleration due to gravity experienced by the rock in meters per second squared ($m/s^2$)?

**A.** $0.0\ m/s^2$

**B.** $9.8\ m/s^2$

**C.** $14.7\ m/s^2$

**D.** $19.6\ m/s^2$

**38.** Imagine a sky diver leaping from a plane. Which of the following statements is not supported by the results of the experiments?

**F.** The diver would be traveling at less than 19.6 m/s downward after falling for 2 s.

**G.** The diver can reduce the time of her trip to the ground by curling tightly into a ball.

**H.** The diver would fall with a greater acceleration if her mass were larger.

**J.** During each second that the diver falls, she travels a greater distance than during the previous second.

**39.** The acceleration due to gravity is dependent on mass and on distance. Why do the rock and the feather have the same acceleration in Figure 1?

**A.** The acceleration is caused by forces in addition to gravity.

**B.** The rock and the feather must have the same mass if they have the same acceleration.

**C.** The acceleration is proportional to the mass of Earth, which is the same in each case, and not to the masses of the objects.

**D.** The acceleration is the same only at the particular distance from Earth's surface at which the scientist conducted the experiment.

**40.** How could the students modify their experimental design to more closely replicate the results of the scientist's study on the effect of gravity on falling objects?

**F.** Drop two feathers that have different shapes but the same mass

**G.** Drop two steel bearings that have different masses

**H.** Drop the rock and the feather from a first floor window

**J.** Throw the rock and the feather toward the ground initially

# ACT Practice Test 3

Name Date

# Practice Test 3

## Passage I

Almost 100 years ago, the astronomers Hertzsprung and Russell began making scatter-plot graphs that compared the luminosity of a star with its surface temperature. They saw that stars were not evenly distributed over the graphs, but that most stars formed a curved band which we now call the *main sequence*. Stars that were located in a separate cluster located above and to the right of the main sequence were labeled *giants*. The result of their studies is shown in Figure 1.

Stars vary in brightness. The amount of light that reaches Earth from a star corresponds to its *magnitude*. The magnitudes of a few stars are shown in Figure 2. Magnitude is an inverse exponential function, so stars that have small magnitudes appear brighter than stars that have larger magnitudes. In order to compare stars with one another, however, the brightness as seen from Earth is not useful data. The magnitude of a star depends on distance to the star as well as the brightness of the star. In order to compare stars, scientists use *absolute magnitude*, which corresponds to relative brightness as viewed from a uniform distance.

Scientists have concluded that main-sequence stars generate heat and light by fusing hydrogen into helium. Scientists predict that stars close to the mass of our sun can continue in their hydrogen-fusion stage for 10 billion years. More massive stars will have shorter lives. On the other hand, stars that are less massive than the sun have longer lives and tend to be found at the lower right of the main sequence on a Hertzsprung-Russell diagram.

When a star about the size of our sun has used up almost all of its hydrogen, its core contracts. Hydrogen fusion continues in the outer shell, and the outer shell expands and cools. These stars begin to glow with a reddish color and are known as *red giants*. Stars that are more massive than the sun grow even larger than giants. They often become 100 or more times larger than the sun. Some stars, like Betelgeuse, grow to 1,000 times greater than the size of the sun. However, because their surface areas have expanded, their surface temperatures are relatively cool.

When a star cannot generate any more energy through fusion, it will eventually shrink. Scientists predict that a star that has a mass close to the sun's mass will shrink until it is about the size of Earth. A star at this stage is called a *white dwarf*. It will cool down over billions of years and gradually fade. However, stars more than 8 times the mass of the sun will contract into very dense neutron stars or into black holes The gravitational pull of a black hole is so great that not even light can escape from it.

Name Date

# Practice Test 3 *continued*

**Figure 1**

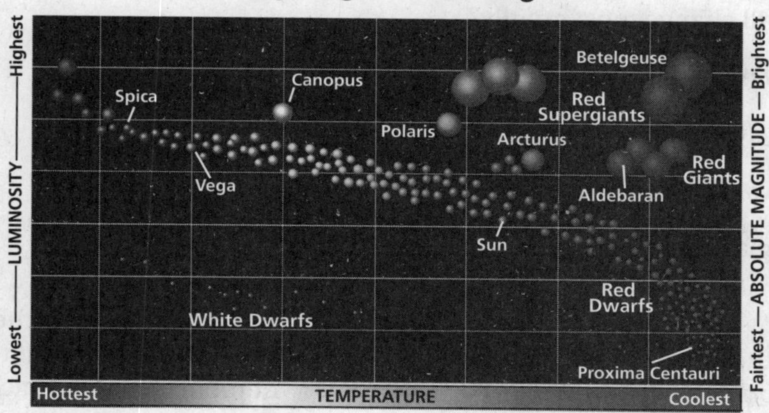


**Figure 2**

**Stellar Characteristics**

| Name | Color | Magnitude | Distance |
|---|---|---|---|
| Arcturus | orange | 0.0 | 36.8 ly |
| Betelgeuse | red | 0.5 | 400ly |
| Canopus | yellow-white | −0.6 | 310 ly |
| Capella | yellow | 0.1 | 42.2 ly |
| Mintaka | blue-violet | 2.2 | 915 ly |
| Rigel | blue-white | 0.2 | 800 ly |
| Sirius | white | −1.4 | 8.6 ly |
| Vega | white | 0.0 | 25.3 ly |

**1.** Which of these stages of a star's lifespan is NOT located on the Hertzsprung-Russell diagram in Figure 1?

**A.** Main sequence

**B.** Red giant

**C.** White dwarf

**D.** Nebula

**2.** Antares is a star that is 60,000 times brighter than the sun, but scientists have concluded that it has run out of hydrogen at its core and is much cooler than the sun is. Where is this star located on the Hertzsprung-Russell diagram in Figure 1?

**F.** Upper left section

**G.** Upper right section

**H.** Lower right section

**J.** Lower left section

Name Date

# Practice Test 3 *continued*

**3.** Which group of stars on the Hertzsprung-Russell diagram in Figure 1 will change most rapidly?

**A.** Yellow main-sequence stars

**B.** White dwarfs

**C.** Red dwarfs

**D.** Supergiants

**4.** Which of these stars would appear to be the brightest if they were observed from a point that is equally distant from each star?

**F.** Betelgeuse

**G.** Canopus

**H.** Vega

**J.** Arcturus

**5.** Which hypothesis best explains why so many stars are on the lower right side of the main sequence in the Hertzsprung-Russell diagram in Figure 1?

**A.** These stars are easier to detect than giants and supergiants.

**B.** These stars have a long life and so there are many in existence at a particular time.

**C.** These stars have greater luminosity so they are easier to observe than stars like the sun.

**D.** These stars are very like the sun, so they are very close by.

**6.** Which of these stars appears to be the brightest in the night sky?

**F.** Betelgeuse

**G.** Canopus

**H.** Vega

**J.** Arcturus

**7.** Which statement is the best conclusion to draw if the relative number of stars in each part of the Hertzsprung-Russell diagram in Figure 1 stayed the same for billions of years?

**A.** Old stars are getting new sources of hydrogen.

**B.** New stars are being created continually.

**C.** The stars on the diagram are moving toward Earth.

**D.** Stars do not change over time.

Name Date

# Practice Test 3 *continued*

## Passage II

Evidence exists that during the millions of years in which the Grand Canyon formed, the canyon divided a single population of tassel-eared squirrels into two populations. One of these squirrel populations, the Kaibab squirrel, now lives on the North Rim of the canyon in isolation from the other tassel-eared squirrels. The other population, the Abert's squirrel, lives on the South Rim. Some biologists think that the two populations of squirrels have evolved into two separate species. Other biologists think that the Kaibab squirrel is a subspecies of the Abert's squirrel.

**Figure 1**

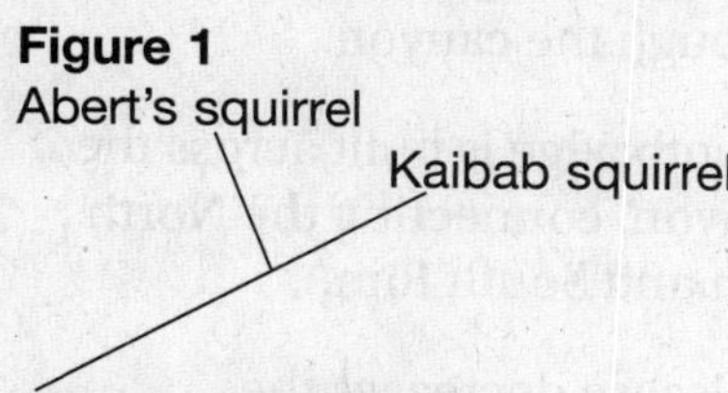


**Figure 2**

| Feature | Abert's squirrel | Kaibab squirrel |
|---|---|---|
| Range | Western United States; Mexico | North Rim's Kaibab Plateau |
| Habitat | Ponderosa pine forest | Ponderosa pine forest |
| Belly | White | Black |
| Tail | White | White |
| Ears | Tasseled | Tasseled |
| Predators | Hawks; Human hunters | Hawks |

Name ______________________________ Date ______________

## Practice Test 3 *continued*

**8.** According to the information in Figure 2, a ban hunting squirrels would most likely cause

**F.** an increase in Abert's squirrels.

**G.** an increase in Kaibab squirrels.

**H.** a decrease in the hawk population.

**J.** a decrease in the poderosa pine population.

**9.** Researchers have found that the Abert's squirrel population on the South Rim fluctuates from year to year, increasing one year and decreasing the next. Which of the following factors would cause the squirrel population to grow?

**A.** Emigration is greater than immigration.

**B.** Emigration is equal to immigration.

**C.** The birth rate is equal to the death rate.

**D.** The birth rate is greater than the death rate.

**10.** Assuming the two types of squirrels can interbreed, which event would *most* likely cause a decrease in the genetic variation between the two types of squirrels?

**F.** A dam is built down stream of the canyon.

**G.** A flood enlarges the river through the canyon.

**H.** A footbridge is built across the canyon, connecting the North Rim and South Rim.

**J.** A disease decreases the population of hawks around the canyon.

# Practice Test 3 *continued*

**11.** Which of the following would provide the best support for the claim that the two types of squirrels had become separate species?

**A.** The two types of squirrels' ears grow tufts of different lengths.

**B.** The two types of squirrels nest at different heights in pines trees.

**C.** The two types of squirrels prefer different foods.

**D.** The two types of squirrels can no longer interbreed.

**12.** The cladogram in Figure 1 shows the evolution of the original tassel-eared squirrel population into two separate species. Which of the following factors would make the evolution of the squirrel population into separate species *less* likely?

**F.** Different predators live on the North Rim than live on the South Rim of the canyon.

**G.** A few of the squirrels manage to cross the canyon and breed with squirrels on the other side.

**H.** Different trees grow on the North Rim than grow on the South Rim of the canyon because of differences in the water table.

**J.** A disease kills most of the squirrels on one side of the canyon, but the squirrels on the other side of the canyon are not affected.

Name Date



**Passage III**

The device shown in Figure 1 is equipped with pressure and temperature sensors. A valve separates the two chambers. When the valve is opened, the two chambers are joined by the tube.

**Figure 1**

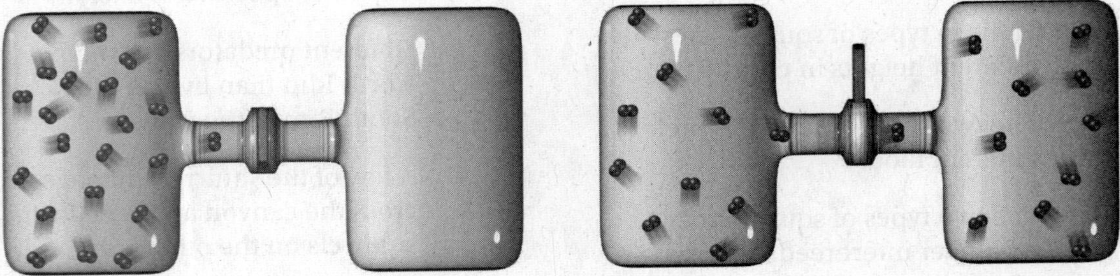

*Experiment 1*

In the first experiment, researchers filled one chamber with gas and removed all the gas from the second chamber. The researchers maintained the gas at a constant temperature as they measured the pressure in each chamber, opened the valve, and measured the pressure again. The experiment was repeated using different-sized chambers, and the results are shown in Table 1.

Table 1

| Volume Versus Pressure Experiment | | | | | |
|---|---|---|---|---|---|
| Chamber 1 | | | Chamber 2 | | |
| Volume (L) | Initial Pressure (kPa) | Final Pressure (kPa) | Volume (L) | Initial Pressure (kPa) | Final Pressure (kPa) |
| 1.0 | 4,960 | 2,480 | 1.0 | 0 | 2,480 |
| 1.0 | 4,960 | 1,240 | 3.0 | 0 | 1,240 |
| 1.0 | 4,960 | 827 | 5.0 | 0 | 827 |

*Experiment 2*

In the second experiment, only one chamber was used. Researchers filled the chamber with gas and measured the temperature and pressure of the gas. The chamber was heated, and the temperature and pressure were recorded over time. The results are shown in Table 2.

Table 2

| Temperature Versus Pressure Experiment | | |
|---|---|---|
| Temperature (°C) | Temperature (K) | Pressure (kPa) |
| 0 | 273 | 1,000 |
| 20 | 293 | 1,073 |
| 40 | 313 | 1,147 |
| 100 | 373 | 1,366 |
| 175 | 448 | 1,641 |
| 273 | 546 | 2,000 |

**13.** Which statement best describes what happens when the valve is opened in the apparatus shown in Figure 1?

**A.** Gas particles are constantly moving and do not tend to attract each other, so a gas expands to fill the volume available to it.

**B.** The gas particles are attracted to the empty container, so they expand to fill it.

**C.** Gas particles begin to move faster when volume is increased, so they fill the empty container.

**D.** Gravity causes the particles in the upper part of the full chamber to fall into the lower part of the empty chamber.

**14.** Based on the results of Experiment 1, which of the following statements could explain the effect of a change in volume on the pressure of a gas in a closed container?

**F.** When the volume is increased, the frequency of collisions increases between gas particles and the container walls, so the pressure decreases.

**G.** As the volume increases, the gas particles expand so they create less pressure inside the container.

**H.** The particles of gas move at a slower rate when the volume increases which causes the pressure to decrease.

**J.** As the gas particles move to occupy the extra volume the pressure decreases because the particles collide against a larger surface area.

# Practice Test 3 *continued*

**15.** Table 1 shows the effect that changing the volume of a gas has on the pressure of the gas. Analyze the data to determine which of these statements best describes the results.

**A.** Pressure is directly proportional to volume.

**B.** Pressure is inversely proportional to volume.

**C.** Based on this experiment, pressure is not related to volume.

**D.** No relationship can be determined without knowing the temperature as well.

**16.** Based on the results of Experiment 2, what is the relationship of the pressure of a gas to its temperature?

**F.** The pressure of a gas is inversely proportional to the Celsius temperature.

**G.** The pressure of a gas is directly proportional to the Kelvin temperature.

**H.** The pressure of a gas shows no relationship to temperature changes in either the Celsius or the Kelvin scale.

**J.** The pressure of a gas increases as a result of a decrease in temperature in either the Celsius or the Kelvin scale.

**17.** Based on the data shown in Table 2, which pair of values is NOT correct?

**A.** –173°C; 100 K

**B.** 30°C; 303 K

**C.** 300°C; 3,030 K

**D.** 127°C; 400K

**18.** A 1 mol sample of oxygen was placed into the apparatus as shown in the first image in Figure 1. After the valve was opened, the gas pressure was measured to be 450 kPa. Based on the results of Experiment 1, what pressure did this amount of gas exert before the valve was opened?

**F.** 225 kPa

**G.** 450 kPa

**H.** 900 kPa

**J.** 1,350 kPa

**19.** Researchers use the apparatus in Figure 1 to study diffusion. Which of the following statements about diffusion of gases is NOT true?

**A.** Diffusion is due to the fast motion of gas molecules.

**B.** Diffusion eventually results in a homogenous mixture of the substances.

**C.** Diffusion occurs as gases move from an area of higher concentration to an area of lower concentration.

**D.** Diffusion involves a decrease in entropy.

Name Date

# Practice Test 3 *continued*

**Passage IV**

Astronomers have concluded that our solar system formed from a swirling cloud of gas and dust about 4.6 billion years ago. The swirling cloud flattened to become a disk, and the sun formed at the center. Each planet formed from that same disk but at different distances from the sun. Astronomers are less certain about how Earth's moon formed. The material of the moon's crust is similar to that of Earth's crust, but the moon as a whole is not nearly as dense as Earth is. That would indicate that metals such as iron and nickel make up a smaller proportion of the moon's composition than they make up of Earth's composition, which further suggests that the moon has a much smaller core in proportion to Earth's core. An explanation for the moon's formation must account for these observations as well as for the fact that the moon orbits Earth very close to the plane of Earth's path around the sun, called the *ecliptic*. Three theories about the origin of the moon are described below.

*Theory 1*

The moon formed from materials removed from Earth's crust and mantle. This is the collisional-ejection theory, which is generally accepted by astronomers today. After Earth formed, a huge object, perhaps as large as the planet Mars, collided with Earth. The energy from the impact tipped Earth on its axis, accounting for the angle of Earth's rotation in relation to the ecliptic. This impact ejected a huge mass of rock and vaporized material into space, which formed a ring around Earth near the ecliptic plane. Gravity pulled this material together to form the moon.

*Theory 2*

A second theory concludes that the moon and Earth formed separately and then came together. This is the capture theory, which states that the moon was once a large asteroid that passed near Earth and was captured by the planet's gravity. This process is thought to account for moons around other planets including the two moons of Mars—Phobos and Deimos.

*Theory 3*

A third theory concludes that Earth and the moon formed together at about the same time from the original disk-shaped cloud of gas and dust. This is known as the co-formation theory. This theory would explain why the moon's orbit is in the same plane as Earth's orbit.

## Practice Test 3 *continued*

**20.** Evidence, such as moon rocks retrieved by astronauts, indicates that the surface materials of the moon are similar to Earth's upper mantle. How does this evidence relate to the theories of the moon's formation?

**F.** This evidence refutes the collisional-ejection theory because the theory requires that the moon be made of exactly the same materials as Earth, not just its mantle.

**G.** The fact that materials that make up the moon are like Earth's upper mantle is strong evidence supporting the collisional-ejection theory because the collision would likely eject material mostly from the upper layers of Earth.

**H.** This evidence most strongly supports the co-formation theory because it indicates that the upper parts of each body formed at the same time.

**J.** This evidence tends to support the capture theory because asteroids formed at the same time as Earth formed so they would likely be similar in composition to Earth.

**21.** Most asteroids contain either rocky material that is different from the rocks in Earth's crust or large amounts of iron. Comets are generally made of ice and other materials that have a low boiling point. How does this evidence relate to the theories of the moon's formation?

**F.** The evidence supports the capture theory because large asteroids are more likely to be similar in composition to Earth than smaller asteroids or comets are.

**G.** The evidence supports none of the theories because all of the material in the solar system is made of the same elements even though there is variation in their distribution.

**H.** The evidence supports the co-formation theory because the observation demonstrates that there is a great deal of variation among bodies in the solar system, so the moon could not be expected to match the composition of Earth exactly.

**J.** The evidence supports none of the theories, but it does refute the capture theory because the composition of the moon does not match the composition of asteroids or comets.

Name Date

# Practice Test 3 *continued*

**22.** Which phenomenon on Earth could be used as supporting evidence for the formation of the moon being caused by a collision between Earth and another large body?

**A.** The relationship between tides and the moon's position

**B.** Volcanic activity around the Pacific Ocean

**C.** The jet stream and other large motions of air within the atmosphere

**D.** The existence of seasons due to the angle of Earth's axis

**23.** Unlike Earth, the moon has almost no atmosphere. How does this fact relate to the three moon formation theories?

**A.** The moon's thin atmosphere supports the co-formation theory because the greater gravitational attraction of Earth caused gases to be pulled toward Earth instead of toward the moon.

**B.** The moon's thin atmosphere supports the capture theory because, like the moon, asteroids do not have an atmosphere.

**C.** The moon's thin atmosphere supports the collisional-ejection theory because material from Earth was ejected into space, where there is no atmosphere.

**D.** The moon's thin atmosphere is not related to any of the formation theories but to the moon's smaller gravitational field that allows gases to escape into space.

**24.** The moon has an iron core. Theories 1 and 3 would be weakened and Theory 2 would be strengthened if which of the following statements were found to be true?

**F.** An asteroid that has an iron core and a rocky outer layer is discovered.

**G.** An iron core forms from molten materials naturally because the denser iron sinks to the center of the mass before the material solidifies.

**H.** The formation of an iron core happens only during the initial formation of a body from the original disk-shaped cloud of gas and dust.

**J.** Material ejected at any direction from a planetary body settles into an orbit in the same plane as the planet's orbit.

# Practice Test 3 *continued*

## Passage V

G. F. Gause, a Russian biologist, experimented with protists that competed for the same food supply and found that the more efficient competitor drove the other to extinction. This effect of one species on another in an ecosystem is called *competitive exclusion.*

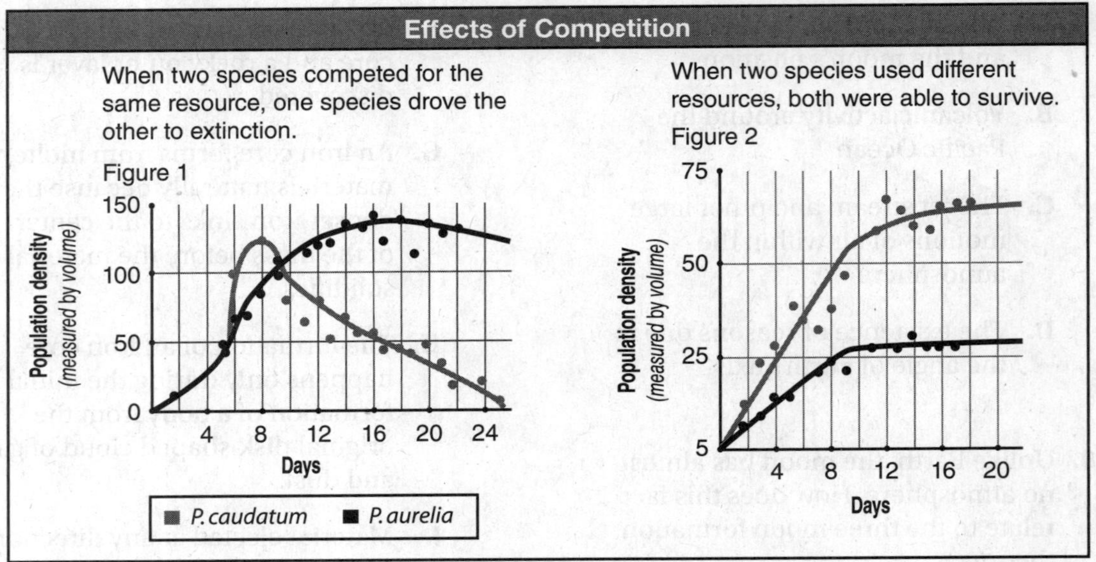


In Figure 1, you can see that when two species competed for the same resource, one species drove the other to extinction. In Figure 2, you can see that when two species used different resources both were able to survive.

Biologists speculate that in the mid-1980s, a cargo ship from eastern Europe dumped ballast water containing a tiny organism called the zebra mussel into the Great Lakes. The zebra mussel is native to waters in eastern Europe but had never lived in North America. The zebra mussels began to attach to piers, boat hulls, pipes, and any other available surface. Zebra mussels prefer attaching to surfaces in water that is 2 to 7 feet deep but have been found at depths of 180 feet in water temperatures ranging from 7°C to 32°C. They live mainly in fresh water with salinities (salt concentrations) of 0.21 to 1.47 parts per thousand (ppt), but they can live in estuaries with salinities up to 13.40 ppt. Thus, conditions in the Great Lakes were ideal for these filter feeders, which strain plankton out of lake water. Plankton is a food resource for other small aquatic animals and fish larvae. Zebra mussels can strain food from about one liter of water per day. These invaders thrived in and spread throughout the Great Lakes. They now threaten other North American waterways. For example, the zebra mussel seems to be out-competing the native mussel in the Hudson River. Figure 3 on the following page shows a decline in the population of native mussels since the zebra mussel was introduced.

Name Date

# Practice Test 3 *continued*

**Figure 3**

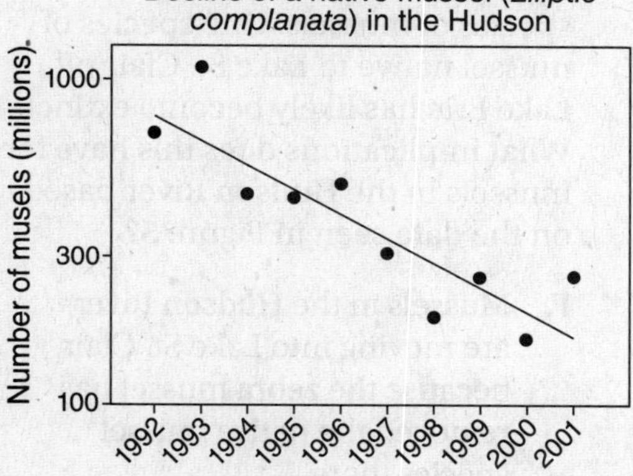


**25.** The presence of large quantities of plankton decreases water clarity. Since zebra mussels were introduced, the clarity of Lake Erie's water has increased 600%. What does this *most likely* indicate about zebra mussels?

**A.** Zebra mussels could be used to solve water pollution problems.

**B.** There is no obvious link between zebra mussels and water clarity.

**C.** Zebra mussels are such efficient feeders that they have greatly reduced the amount of plankton in Lake Erie.

**D.** In clear water, it is easy for zebra mussels to catch and kill other mussel species.

**26.** Which statement about the zebra mussel invasion is best supported by the data in Figures 1 and 2?

**F.** Zebra mussels can coexist with other Great Lakes species because they do not compete for the same resources.

**G.** Even though zebra mussels compete for resources with other species, the Great Lakes are so big that there is plenty of food for all organisms.

**H.** Zebra mussels are a good food resource for other animals in the Great Lakes, so many aquatic animal populations should increase.

**J.** Because plankton forms the base of the aquatic food chain, zebra mussels could cause the extinction of other species that depend on plankton as a resource.

## Practice Test 3 *continued*

**27.** The increased clarity of water in the Great Lakes can have far-reaching effects on this freshwater community. What would *most likely* be the first change to happen?

**A.** Sunlight penetrates to greater depths and causes an increased growth of algae.

**B.** The number of scuba divers increases and causes damage to lake-bottom ecosystems.

**C.** Fish see their prey at greater distances and become more efficient feeders.

**D.** Ultraviolet light reaches deeper under water and causes more cases of cancer in fish.

**28.** Based on the information in the passage above, which variables best determine where the zebra mussel can exist?

**A.** Availability of surfaces for attachment, water depth, water salinity, availability of plankton

**B.** Water clarity, availability of native mussel species, water temperature, water salinity

**C.** Availability of ballast water, water salinity, water depth, water temperature

**D.** Water depth, availability of fish larvae, water clarity, availability of plankton

**29.** Zebra mussels have severely diminished the populations of other species of mussels. One species of mussel native to Lake St. Clair off Lake Erie has likely become extinct. What implications does this have for mussels in the Hudson River based on the data seen in Figure 3?

**F.** Mussels in the Hudson River are moving into Lake St. Clair because the zebra mussel has removed the native mussel species there.

**G.** Mussels in the Hudson River are decreasing in numbers and could be wiped out by zebra mussels as the mussel species in Lake St. Clair is suspected to have been.

**H.** Mussels in the Hudson River are increasing in numbers as a result of competitive pressure from zebra mussels.

**J.** Mussels in the Hudson River have likely been overharvested and the decline in numbers should not be seen as being connected to the introduction of zebra mussels.

# Practice Test 3 *continued*

**Passage VI**

In a correctly written chemical equation, the law of conservation of mass is observed. That means that mass is neither created nor destroyed. A balanced chemical equation shows this by having the same number of each type of atom on both sides of the equation.

Thousands of known chemical reactions occur in living systems, in industrial processes, and in chemical laboratories. Often it is necessary to predict the products formed in one of these reactions. Memorizing the products formed in every one of the known chemical reactions would be an impossible task. It is therefore more realistic and more useful to classify reactions based on similarities in the changes that occur. This general information about reaction types can then be used to predict the products of specific reactions.

There are several ways to classify chemical reactions. One classification scheme, shown in Table 1, describes five basic types of reactions.

**Table 1: Types of Chemical Reactions**

| Reaction | General Equation |
|---|---|
| **Synthesis** | $A + X \rightarrow AX$ |
| **Decomposition** | $AX \rightarrow A + X$ |
| **Single-displacement** | $A + BX \rightarrow AX + B$<br>$Y + BX \rightarrow BY + X$ |
| **Double-displacement** | $AX + BY \rightarrow AY + BX$ |
| **Combustion** | reactants include $O_2$ |

The ability of elements or compounds to undergo chemical reactions varies greatly. In fact, some combinations of reactants will not undergo a chemical reaction. An activity series organizes elements according to their reactivity. Table 2 shows an activity series for metals. In general, a single-displacement reaction will occur only when a more-reactive element (one that is higher in the series) is placed into a solution of an ionic compound of a less-reactive element (one that is lower in the series). During the reaction, electrons are transferred from the metal atoms to the positive ions of the metal in solution. As a result, the more-reactive metal atoms turn into positive ions in solution and the less-reactive metal ions change into metal atoms.

**Table 2: Activity of metals**

| Metals | Activity |
|---|---|
| Li<br>Rb<br>K<br>Ba<br>Sr<br>Ca<br>Na | React with cold $H_2O$ and acids, replacing hydrogen. React with oxygen, forming oxides. |
| Mg<br>Al<br>Mn<br>Zn<br>Cr<br>Fe<br>Cd | React with steam (but not cold water) and acids, replacing hydrogen. React with oxygen, forming oxides. |
| Co<br>Ni<br>Sn<br>Pb | Do not react with water. React with acids, replacing hydrogen. React with oxygen, forming oxides. |
| $H_2$<br>Sb<br>Bi<br>Cu<br>Hg | React with oxygen, forming oxides. |
| Ag<br>Pt<br>Au | Fairly unreactive, forming oxides only indirectly. |

Name Date

# Practice Test 3 *continued*

**30.** During a combustion reaction, propane ($C_3H_8$) is changed into carbon dioxide and water. Based on Table 1, which of the following is the correctly balanced equation for this reaction?

**F.** $C_3H_8 \rightarrow 3CO_2 + 4H_2O$

**G.** $3CO_2 + 4H_2O \rightarrow C_3H_8 + 5O_2$

**H.** $C_3H_8 + 5O_2 \rightarrow 3CO_2 + 4H_2O$

**J.** $C_3H_8 + 3CO_2 \rightarrow 2O_2 + 2H_2O$

**31.** Which of the following is a balanced chemical equation for a synthesis reaction?

**A.** $Na + Cl_2 \rightarrow NaCl$

**B.** $2Fe + O_2 \rightarrow Fe_2O_3$

**C.** $2H_2 + O_2 \rightarrow 2H_2O$

**D.** $2Zn + 2HCl \rightarrow ZnCl_2 + H_2$

**32.** Which of the following is NOT a balanced chemical equation?

**F.** $2ZnS + 3O_2 \rightarrow 2ZnO + SO_2$

**G.** $Fe_2O_3 + 3CO \rightarrow 2Fe + 3CO_2$

**H.** $Na_2SiF_6 + 4Na \rightarrow Si + 6NaF$

**J.** $2NH_3 + 3CuO \rightarrow N_2 + 3Cu + 3H_2O$

**33.** Under certain conditions, ammonia ($NH_3$) combines with oxygen ($O_2$) to form nitrogen monoxide (NO) and water ($H_2O$). Based on Table 1, what type of chemical reaction does this describe?

**A.** Synthesis

**B.** Decomposition

**C.** Double-displacement

**D.** Combustion

**34.** Based on Table 2 and the information in the passage above, which of the following correctly describes the reaction between the metal and the aqueous solution provided?

**F.** Electrons are transferred from atoms of silver metal to the chromium(III) ions in a solution of chromium(III) nitrate.

**G.** Electrons are transferred from atoms of zinc metal to the copper(II) ions in a solution of copper(II) sulfate.

**H.** Electrons are transferred from aluminum ions in a solution of aluminum chloride to atoms of aluminum metal.

**J.** Electrons are transferred from lithium ions in a solution of lithium hydroxide to atoms of magnesium metal.

**35.** When sodium metal is dropped into water, a violent reaction occurs and a flammable product forms. Based on the information in Tables 1 and 2, what type of chemical reaction occurs, and what is the flammable material that is produced?

**A.** Single-displacement; hydrogen

**B.** Combustion; oxygen

**C.** Double-displacement; sodium hydroxide

**D.** Decomposition; sodium hydrate

# Practice Test 3 *continued*

## Passage VII

A group of students conducted experiments in their science lab to explore magnetic fields.

*Experiment 1*
In the first experiment, the students used a small compass to map the magnetic field around a bar magnet. They placed the compass near a bar magnet at a number of positions and then drew the map of the magnetic field, which is shown in Figure 1.

**Figure 1** **Figure 2**

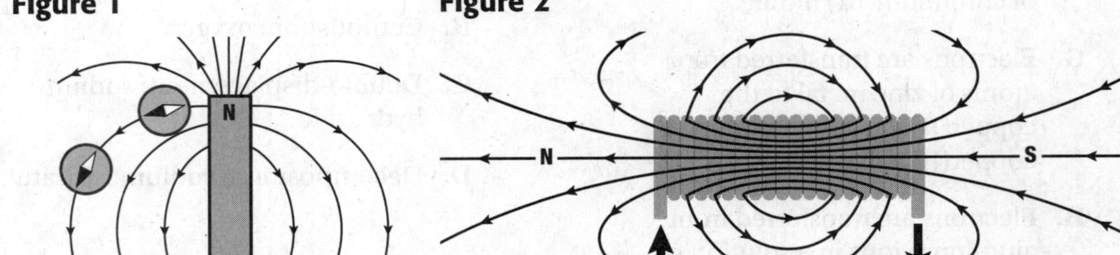


*Experiment 2*
In the second experiment, the students used copper wire to construct a solenoid, like the one in Figure 2. They measured the strength of the magnetic field of the solenoid by determining the maximum distance at which the solenoid caused a small steel ball to roll toward it. The students explored how changes in the number of coils and the amount of applied voltage affect the strength of the field. Their results are recorded in Table 1.

**Table 1 Relative Magnetic Field Strength of a Solenoid**

| Number of coils | Number of batteries | Maximum distance to attract ball (cm) |
|---|---|---|
| 5 | 1 | 2 |
| 20 | 1 | 8 |
| 20 | 2 | 15 |
| 20 | 3 | 23 |
| 30 | 1 | 12 |
| 30 | 2 | 25 |

**36.** A compass is placed inside the solenoid in Figure 2. How would the dark (north-seeking) end of the compass behave when the compass was at the center of the solenoid?

**F.** It would point toward the left end of the solenoid that is marked N.

**G.** It would point toward the right end of the solenoid that is marked S.

**H.** It would alternately point toward the left end of the solenoid and toward the right end of the solenoid.

**J.** It would continuously rotate in a full circle without stopping in a single orientation.

**37.** What is the source of the magnetic field around the solenoid shown in Figure 2?

**A.** The magnetic materials used to make the wire of the solenoid coils

**B.** The motion of electrically charged particles in the wire

**C.** The vibrating motion of the wire coils when a current exists in them

**D.** The effect of Earth's magnetic field on the copper wire

**38.** A battery that is attached to the wire causes the current in the solenoid in Figure 2. What effect would reversing the battery have on the solenoid?

**F.** Reversing the battery would reverse the current but would have no effect on the magnetic field.

**G.** Reversing the battery would reverse the direction of both the current and the magnetic field.

**H.** Reversing the battery would decrease the current and increase the magnetic field strength.

**J.** Reversing the battery would reverse the current and cancel out the magnetic field.

**39.** Which of the following statements correctly describes the results of Experiment 2?

**A.** The strength of the magnetic field is directly proportional to the number of coils and inversely proportional to the number of batteries.

**B.** The strength of the magnetic field is inversely proportional to the number of coils and inversely proportional to the number of batteries.

**C.** The strength of the magnetic field is inversely proportional to the number of coils and directly proportional to the number of batteries.

**D.** The strength of the magnetic field is directly proportional to the number of coils and directly proportional to the number of batteries.

**40.** Based on the results of Experiment 2, which of the following conditions should be able to attract the steel ball from a distance of 24 cm?

**F.** 10 coils and 5 batteries

**G.** 15 coils and 4 batteries

**H.** 25 coils and 2 batteries

**J.** 40 coils and 1 battery

# ACT Practice Test 4

Name Date

# Practice Test 4

## Passage I

Pure water is an extremely weak electrolyte that undergoes self-ionization to produce hydronium ions and hydroxide ions:

$$H_2O(l) + H_2O(l) \rightleftharpoons H_3O^+(aq) + OH^-(aq)$$

Conductivity measurements show that concentrations of $H_3O^+$ and $OH^-$ (written as $[H_3O^+]$ and $[OH^-]$) in pure water are each only $1.0 \times 10^{-7}$ mol/L of water at 25°C. The ionization constant of water is expressed as $K_w$.

$$K_w = [H_3O^+][OH^-]$$

If the concentration of one of the ions increases, the concentration of the other ion decreases. Solutions in which the $[H_3O^+]$ is greater than the $[OH^-]$ are acidic. Solutions in which the $[OH^-]$ is greater than the $[H_3O^+]$ are basic. At 25°C, the product of the two concentrations is always equal to $1.0 \times 10^{-14}$ mol2/L2. The pH of a solution is calculated using the formula $pH = -\log[H_3O^+]$. Therefore, the pH of neutral water is calculated as follows: $pH = -(\log 1.0 \times 10^{-7}) = 7$.

Acidic substances donate hydrogen ions, which then combine with water molecules to form hydronium ions. The increase in hydronium ion concentration lowers the pH of the solution. Basic substances generally increase the pH by donating hydroxide ions to a solution. When acids and bases react with one another, the hydronium and hydroxide ions combine to form two molecules of water. The second product of the neutralization reaction of an acid and a base is a salt, an ionic compound made up of the anion from the acid and the cation from the base.

*Experiment 1*

A group of students used a pH meter to measure the pH of an unknown solution. They recorded the change in pH as they added a solution of calcium hydroxide to the solution. Their data are shown in Figure 1, plotted as pH versus the number of moles ' of $Ca(OH)_2$ added.

Figure 1

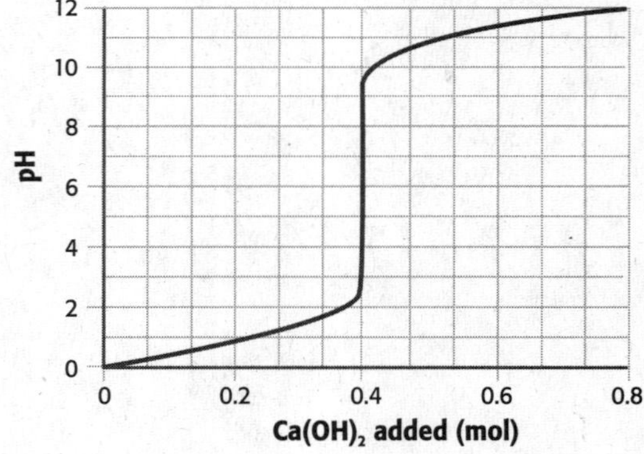

Name Date

# Practice Test 4 *continued*

*Experiment 2*

The students then measured the pH of a number of known substances and arranged their data on in Table 1.

Table 1

**The PH Scale**

| | pH | Substance |
|---|---|---|
| ALKALINE | 14 | Lye |
| | 13 | Caustic Soda |
| | 12 | Lime |
| | 11 | Ammonia |
| | 10 | Magnesium Oxide |
| | 9 | Borax |
| | 8 | Sea Water |
| | 7 | *Deionized Water* |
| ACID | 6 | Milk |
| | 5 | Cottage Cheese |
| | 4 | Carrots |
| | 3 | Vinegar |
| | 2 | Lemon Juice |
| | 1 | Battery Acid |

**1.** Which of the following statements best describes what happened during Experiment 1?

**A.** The students added a basic solution to an acidic solution which caused the pH to increase as the hydronium ion concentration decreased.

**B.** The students added an acidic solution to a basic solution and ended with a neutral solution of a salt in water.

**C.** The pH of the solution increased as the students added a base to an acid because the concentration of hydronium ions increased.

**D.** The pH of the solution decreased as the students added a base to an acid and the concentration of hydronium ions decreased.

**2.** Based on the titration curve shown in Figure 1, how many moles of hydronium ions did the original solution contain?

**F.** 0.20 mole

**G.** 0.40 mole

**H.** 0.80 mole

**J.** 1.0 mole

# Practice Test 4 *continued*

**3.** During the titration shown in Figure 1, the solution reached a point at which the concentration of hydronium ions was exactly equal to the concentration of hydroxide ions. What was the pH of the solution at that point?

**A.** 0

**B.** 2

**C.** 7

**D.** 10

**4.** Based on the information in Figure 2, what is the value of $[H_3O^+]$ in the sample of cottage cheese?

**F.** $1.0 \times 10^{-9}$ M

**G.** $5.0 \times 10^{-7}$ M

**H.** $1.0 \times 10^{-5}$ M

**J.** $5.0 \times 10^{-5}$ M

**5.** Assuming that the data in Figure 2 were collected at 25°C, calculate the product $[H_3O^+][OH^-]$ for lemon juice.

**F.** $2.0 \times 10^{-7}$ M$^2$

**G.** $1.0 \times 10^{-2}$ M$^2$

**H.** $1.0 \times 10^{-7}$ M$^2$

**J.** $1.0 \times 10^{-14}$ M$^2$

**6.** The pOH of a solution can be calculated from the concentration of hydroxide ions in the solution as follows:

$$pOH = -\log[OH^-]$$

Because the product of the concentrations of hydronium and hydroxide is $1.0 \times 10^{-14}$ M, the sum of pOH and pH is 14. What is the pOH of the ammonia sample shown in Figure 2?

**F.** 0

**G.** 3

**H.** 4

**J.** 11

**7.** The students performed a third experiment, in which they diluted the caustic soda and battery acid solutions whose pH was measured in Experiment 2. Then they combined the two solutions to form a neutral solution. If they started with10 mL of battery acid, how much lye solution did they need?

**A.** 1 mL

**B.** 10 mL

**C.** 50 mL

**D.** 100 mL

# Practice Test 4 *continued*

**Passage II**

Autotrophs use photosynthesis to produce organic compounds from carbon dioxide ($CO_2$) and water. The oxygen ($O_2$) and some of the organic compounds produced are then used by cells in a process called *cellular respiration.*

Photosynthesis is summarized by the equation:
$6CO_2 + 6H_2O + \textit{Light energy} \rightarrow C_6H_{12}O_6 + 6O_2$

Environmental factors affect the rate of photosynthesis in plants. For example, as shown in Figure 1, as temperature increases, the rate of photosynthesis increases to a maximum, but then decreases.

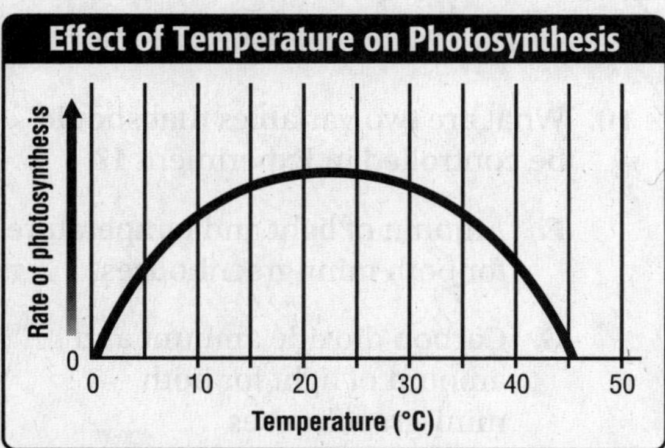


**Figure 1**

*Experiment 1*

Increased $CO_2$ levels also affect photosynthesis and subsequent plant growth. To investigate the effect of increased $CO_2$ levels on plant growth, a scientist conducted the following experiment with tomato plants. First, two mini-greenhouses were set up with identical components. One was labeled *A,* and the other labeled *B.* In mini-greenhouse B, a carbon dioxide delivery system was installed. Thirty 2-week old tomato seedlings were purchased, and their initial masses were recorded. Then, the seedlings were divided into two groups of 15 seedlings, and one group was transplanted into each mini-greenhouse. The $CO_2$ concentrations in both mini-greenhouses were recorded. The $CO_2$ concentration in mini-greenhouse B was increased so that it was twice the level found in mini-greenhouse A. The tomato plants were observed at weeks 3, 5, 7, 10, and 13. During each observation, each plant was measured, and the average mass was calculated and recorded in Table 1.

# Practice Test 4 *continued*

**Table 1**

**Growth of Tomato Plants in Normal $CO_2$ (Mini-Greenhouse A) and Doubled $CO_2$ (Mini-Greenhouse B) Concentrations Over a 13-week Period**

| Week | Biomass of plant sample for mini-greenhouse A (grams) | Biomass of plant sample for mini-greenhouse B (grams) |
|---|---|---|
| Begin | 2 | 2 |
| 3 | 20 | 30 |
| 5 | 150 | 200 |
| 7 | 200 | 350 |
| 10 | 300 | 550 |
| 13 | 450 | 700 |

**8.** Which of these describes what happens to the light energy absorbed by a plant during photosynthesis?

**F.** It is released as heat during the reaction that converts carbon dioxide and water into glucose and oxygen.

**G.** It is used up during the conversion of carbon dioxide and water into glucose and oxygen.

**H.** It is converted into chemical energy that is stored in the glucose made by the plant.

**J.** It is converted into kinetic energy that is used to transport materials throughout the plant.

**9.** Which variable did the scientist choose as the independent variable in Experiment 1?

**A.** Temperature

**B.** Tomato plant growth

**C.** Amount of water added

**D.** Carbon dioxide level

**10.** What are two variables that should be controlled in Experiment 1?

**F.** Amount of light and temperature for both mini-greenhouses

**G.** Carbon dioxide amount and amount of light for both mini-greenhouses

**H.** Watering schedule and carbon dioxide amount for both mini-greenhouses

**J.** The height and mass of the plants in each mini-greenhouse

**11.** Which variable was the dependent variable in Experiment 1?

**A.** The length of time the investigation took to complete

**B.** The amount of water needed for each mini-greenhouse

**C.** The difference in plant growth

**D.** The intensity of green color in the plants

**12.** Based on the data from Experiment 1, which of these statements is *most likely* true?

**F.** Decreasing the level of carbon dioxide leads to an increase in the biomass of plants.

**G.** Increasing the level of carbon dioxide leads to an increase in the biomass of plants.

**H.** The increased biomass directly relates to the crop yield of the tomato plants.

**J.** The increased biomass caused an increase in the carbon dioxide level.

**13.** Which of the following statements is supported by the data in Figure 1?

**A.** Photosynthesis does not occur at 0°C.

**B.** The rate of photosynthesis is higher at 40°C than it is at 20°C.

**C.** The best temperature for photosynthesis is approximately 46°C.

**D.** The rate of photosynthesis increases as temperature increases from 25°C to 30°C.

**14.** Suppose that in a new experiment using new tomato plants, all variables except temperature were controlled. In this second experiment, the temperature in mini-greenhouse A was held at a constant 20°C, and the temperature in mini-greenhouse B was held at a constant 35°C. According to the data in Figure 1, which of the following statements would *most likely* be true?

**F.** By week 13, the average mass of the plants in mini-greenhouse B would be greater than the average mass of the plants in mini-greenhouse A.

**G.** By week 13, the average mass of the plants in mini-greenhouse A would be greater than the average mass of the plants in mini-greenhouse B.

**H.** By week 13, the average mass of the plants in both mini-greenhouses would be about the same.

**J.** By week 13 the plants in both mini-greenhouses would have died because of the absence of photosynthesis.

# Practice Test 4 *continued*

## Passage III

*Experiment 1*

The first discovery of a subatomic particle resulted from investigations into the relationship between electricity and matter. Before this time, the atom was viewed as not being composed of any smaller particles. In 1897, physicist J. J. Thomson performed an experiment in which he applied an electric current to a cathode-ray tube, as shown in Figure 1. When voltage was applied to the electrodes, the surface of the tube directly opposite the cathode glowed. Scientists hypothesized that the glow was caused by a stream of particles. Thomson exposed the cathode-ray tube to a magnetic field and to an electric field and made the following observations:

1. Cathode rays were deflected by a magnetic field in the opposite direction as an object that has a negative charge is deflected.
2. The rays were deflected away from a negatively charged object.

Figure 1

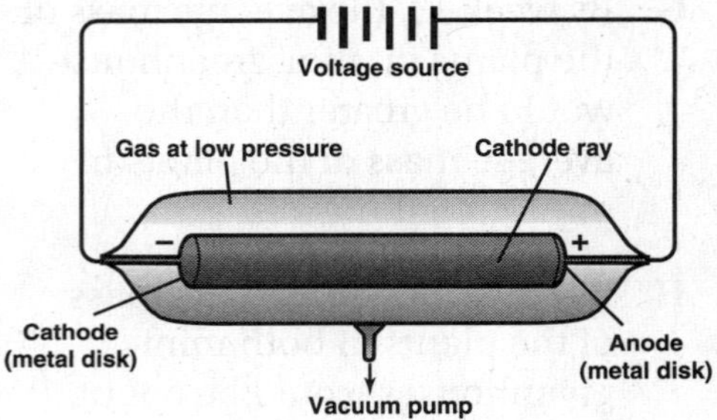


*Experiment 2*

More detail of the atom's structure was provided in 1911 by New Zealander Ernest Rutherford and his associates Hans Geiger and Ernest Marsden. The scientists bombarded a thin piece of gold foil with fast-moving *alpha particles*, which are positively charged particles. Each alpha particle has about four times the mass of a hydrogen atom. Geiger and Marsden assumed that mass and charge were uniformly distributed throughout the atoms of the gold foil. They expected the alpha particles to pass through with only a slight deflection, and for the vast majority of the particles, this was the case. However, when the scientists checked for the possibility of wide-angle deflections, they were shocked to find that roughly 1 in 8,000 of the alpha particles had actually been deflected back toward the source, as shown in Figure 2. As Rutherford later exclaimed, it was "as if you had fired a 15-inch [artillery] shell at a piece of tissue paper and it came back and hit you."

Name Date

# Practice Test 4 *continued*

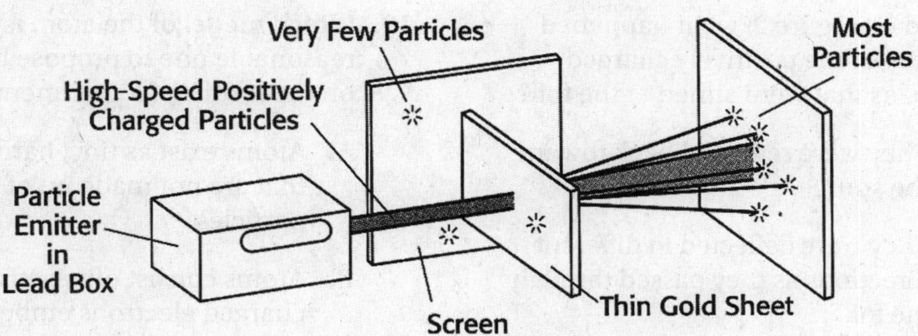


**15.** Which hypothesis below is supported by the results of Experiment 1, Thomson's cathode-ray tube experiment?

**A.** The cathode ray is a stream of positively charged particles that are affected by the magnetic field and by the presence of a charged object.

**B.** The sign of the electric charge of the particles depends on the type of field the cathode ray is exposed to as it travels from one end of the tube to the other.

**C.** The sign of the electric charge of the particles cannot be determined because positive and negative particles are both affected by a magnetic field.

**D.** The cathode ray is a stream of negatively charged particles that are affected by the magnetic field and by the presence of a charged object.

**16.** Which of the following is a conclusion that can be made based on the results of Experiment 1 and the knowledge that atoms are electrically neutral?

**F.** Atoms consist of a combination of electrons, protons, and neutrons.

**G.** Electrons are very small compared to the size of an atom, so they must be located outside the nucleus.

**H.** Atoms consist of a number of positive charges equal to the number of electrons.

**J.** Electrons can exist only as part of an atom and not as separate particles because charges must be balanced.

# Practice Test 4 *continued*

**17.** Based on Figure 2, what happened to most of the positively charged particles that were aimed at the foil?

**A.** They were reflected back toward the source.

**B.** They were deflected in different directions as they passed through the foil.

**C.** They were unaffected in their motion as they passed through the foil.

**D.** They were absorbed by the foil and were not detected.

**18.** Which statement below provides the best explanation of the unexpected result observed in Experiment 2?

**F.** Alpha particles collided with atoms and bounced off of the electron clouds surrounding the nuclei.

**G.** The alpha particles were repelled by small, dense regions of positive charge inside the atoms.

**H.** A positive charge that is evenly distributed throughout the gold foil repelled alpha particles that were moving too slowly to pass through the foil.

**J.** A design flaw in the experiment caused the appearance of particles reflecting back even though none actually did.

**19.** Which model of the atom is a reasonable one to propose based on the results of Experiment 2?

**A.** Atoms exist as tiny, hard balls that are not made up of smaller particles.

**B.** Atoms consist of negatively charged electrons embedded in a positively charged mass like chocolate chips in cookie dough.

**C.** Atoms consist of a small, dense, positively charged nucleus surrounded by orbiting electrons.

**D.** Atoms exist as a nucleus of negatively charged electrons with an equal number of positive charges orbiting around the nucleus.

## Passage IV

Tropical storms are concentrated over a small area when warm moist air over the ocean begins to rise rapidly. As it rises, the water vapor in the air cools and condenses. This phase change from gas to liquid releases a large amount of stored energy that increases the motion and force of the moving air. Due to the motion of the rotating Earth, the winds begin to move in a circular motion rather than in a straight line. This is known as the *Coriolis effect*, and it causes hurricanes to rotate in a counterclockwise direction in the Northern Hemisphere and in a clockwise direction in the Southern Hemisphere. The storm builds strength over warm waters as more energy is released by the rising air. In the center of the storm, dry air sinks and forms a low pressure area known as the *eye*. Inside the eye, the air is calm, and the pressure is low. The low pressure of the eye coupled with the high winds of the hurricane creates a storm surge that causes much of the destruction when the hurricane moves onto land. Because of their high winds and large size, hurricanes are the most destructive storms on Earth. Hurricanes are categorized base on wind speed, pressure, and storm surge. A category 4 or 5 hurricane can cause catastrophic destruction.

**FIGURE 1: CROSS-SECTION OF A HURRICANE**

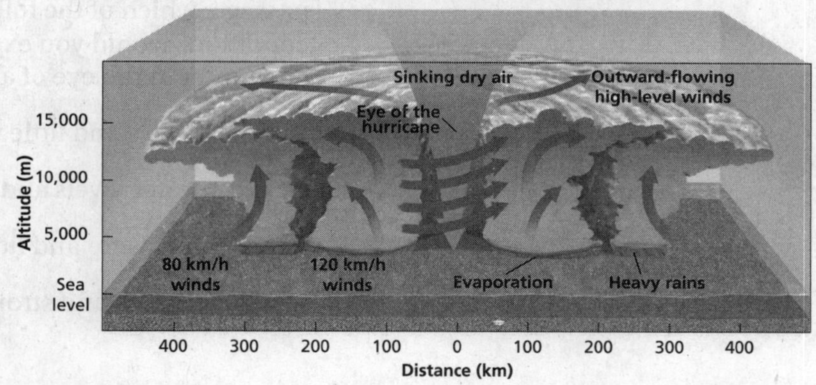


| Saffir-Simpson scale | | | |
|---|---|---|---|
| **Category** | **Winds (kilometers per hour)** | **Pressure (millibars)** | **Surge (meters)** |
| tropical depression | < 62 | - | - |
| tropical storm | 62 – 117 | - | - |
| 1 | 118 – 152 | > 980 | 1.22 – 1.53 |
| 2 | 153 – 176 | 965 – 980 | 1.54 – 2.44 |
| 3 | 177 – 208 | 945 – 965 | 2.45 – 3.66 |
| 4 | 209 – 248 | 920 – 945 | 3.67 – 5.49 |
| 5 | > 249 | < 920 | > 5.50 |

## Practice Test 4 *continued*

**20.** Much of the energy of a hurricane comes from water vapor. From where does the water vapor get its energy?

**F.** Heat that is transferred from the interior of Earth and is absorbed by ocean water

**G.** Friction between particles of water as waves and tides move the water

**H.** Winds that carry energy, cooling the polar regions and warming tropical waters

**J.** Sunlight that is absorbed by water at the surface of the ocean

**21.** Based on Table 1, which of the following conditions is necessary for a storm to be classified as a hurricane on the Saffir-Simpson scale?

**A.** Wind speeds in excess of 117 kilometers per hour

**B.** Air pressure in the eye greater than 980 millibars

**C.** A storm surge of less than 1 meter

**D.** Wind speeds of at least 62 kilometers per hour

**22.** Based on the information in the passage, which of the following conditions would you expect to encounter in the eye of a hurricane?

**F.** Clear skies and little wind

**G.** Low water levels and light rains

**H.** High pressure and little wind

**J.** Heavy rains and strong winds

# Practice Test 4 *continued*

**23.** Based on information in the passage, why do hurricanes generally tend to lose strength and move to a lower classification on the Saffir-Simpson scale shortly after making landfall?

**A.** Mountains on land block the wind and force it to move upward and lose strength.

**B.** Rain that falls on land does not evaporate as quickly as rain that falls on water.

**C.** The air above land tends to be cooler and less moist than the air above tropical oceans is so there is less condensation and therefore less energy to power the storm.

**D.** When the storm surge hits land, most of the energy of the water is absorbed by rock and soil which causes the hurricane to weaken.

**24.** An airplane flying into a hurricane measures the maximum wind speeds as about 190 kilometers per hour. Based on Table 1, how much of a storm surge should weather forecasters predict?

**F.** About 1.22 meters

**G.** Between 1.54 meters and 2.44 meters

**H.** Between 2.45 meters and 3.66 meters

**J.** At least 5.50 meters

Name Date

## Practice Test 4 *continued*

**Passage V**

The gray wolf was exterminated from much of the northwestern United States by the 1920s. To re-establish populations in the mid-1990s, scientists released 64 wolves into Yellowstone National Park and 34 wolves into central Idaho. Two scientists discuss the benefits and problems of reintroducing the wolf.

*Scientist 1*
There is no need to re-introduce wolves, because wolves are not truly endangered. Hundreds of wolves live in Minnesota, and thousands live in Alaska and Canada, so wolves should not receive special treatment as an endangered species. Wolves would interfere with humans' hunting. Both hunters and wolves hunt for large game animals such as deer, elk, or moose. Wolves would create too much competition for the game animals. Hunting is an important part of the economies of the western states. Also, licensed hunting has become part of the way large parks and wildlife preserves are managed. Hunting is sometimes allowed by park and game managers to control wildlife populations. Hunting fees also help fund wildlife management efforts, such as habitat improvement and biological studies. Wolves may also kill livestock on ranches. Even though there is a program to pay ranchers for lost livestock, the program will last only as long as wolves are classified as an endangered species. When there are many wolves again in the target areas, the wolf will no longer have endangered status. The payment program will disappear when it would be needed most. Wolves living in high concentrations near people may pose a threat to people, as well.

*Scientist 2*
The federal government must uphold the law by trying to restore wolf populations in the United States. Furthermore, studies indicate that the reintroduction plan could restore a balance to some western ecosystems. Predation by wolves would keep the herds of elk, moose, and deer from growing too dense and overgrazing the land. Once populations could support hunting wolves, the licensed hunting of wolves, themselves, might help support the reintroduction plans. Populations of both wolves and game animals could be managed. Studies indicate that wolves do not prey on livestock. Most wolves prefer to hunt wild animals rather than domestic animals. Wolves rarely attack livestock when large herds of wild game are nearby. In fact, from 1995 to 1997, fewer than five wolf attacks on livestock were reported in the United States. In response to fears that the wolves pose a danger to humans, supporters say this is also unlikely. There have been no verified attacks on humans by healthy wolves in North America. Wolves are shy animals that prefer to stay away from people.

**25.** Which of the following phrases best describes the major difference between the two scientists' hypotheses?

**A.** The best location for wolf reintroduction

**B.** The timing of wolf reintroduction

**C.** The monitoring of wolf reintroduction

**D.** The safety of wolf reintroduction

**26.** According to Scientist 2's viewpoint, reintroducing wolves could help save federal lands by:

**F.** preventing overgrazing by elk, moose, and deer.

**G.** enabling people to farm safely there.

**H.** reducing the populations of rats and other rodents.

**J.** creating predatory competition for coyotes and panthers.

**27.** Scientist 1's viewpoint indicates that when wolves are no longer officially endangered, ranchers will:

**A.** begin to be compensated for livestock killed by wolves.

**B.** no longer be compensated for livestock killed by wolves.

**C.** have to compensate the federal government for wolves they kill.

**D.** have to compensate the federal government to have hunters kill wolves.

# Practice Test 4 *continued*

**28.** Which of the following statements best describes how Scientist 2 would explain why domestic livestock are safe from reintroduced wolves?

**F.** Wolves are too weak to kill livestock.

**G.** Fences prevent wolves from encountering livestock to kill.

**H.** Wolves prefer to kill wild game.

**J.** Wolves have never killed domestic livestock.

**29.** How does the relationship between wolves and humans in range lands on which livestock are raised affect the overall population of wolves in those areas?

**A.** Competitive exclusion tends to reduce the wolf population.

**B.** Wolves become predatory on humans, increasing the wolf population.

**C.** Humans prey on wolves in order to protect livestock and this reduces the wolf population.

**D.** There is no effect on the wolf population because the wolves and humans have different roles in the ecosystem.

**30.** Scientist 1's viewpoint could be weakened by which of the following observations, if true?

**F.** A study shows that the reintroduction of wolves creates larger, healthier populations of game for hunting.

**G.** A study shows that the reintroduction of wolves creates smaller, weaker populations of game for hunting.

**H.** A study shows that the reintroduction of wolves increases the number of wolf attacks on livestock.

**J.** A study shows that the reintroduction of wolves increases the number of wolf attacks on people.

**Passage VI**

During a laboratory experiment on the properties of light, students shined a laser at a surface and then recorded the position where the reflected beam struck.

*Experiment 1*

In the first experiment, the students shined the light on the surface of a mirror. They recorded the angle between the beam of light coming from the light source and a line perpendicular to the mirror and the angle between the reflected beam of light and the same perpendicular line. They drew Figure 1 to illustrate their observations.

Figure 1

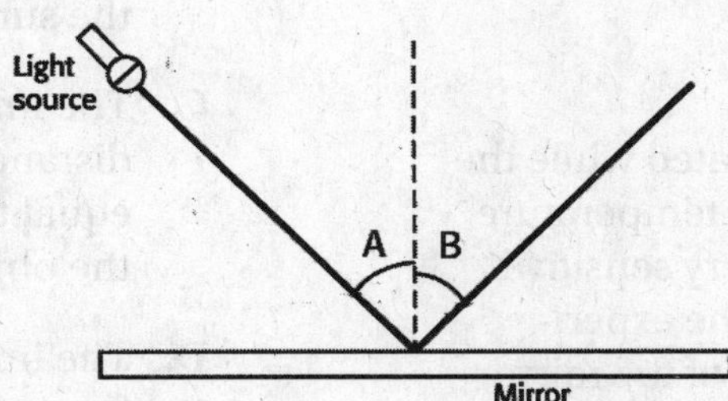


The students also measured the intensity of the light that was reflected from the mirror. When they compared it with the intensity of light that had traveled the same distance through air, without reflection, they found that the reflected light was not quite as bright. Two different hypotheses were proposed to explain the loss of light intensity.

Hypothesis A

Some of the light was absorbed by the mirror because no surface is a perfect reflector. Some light is always absorbed when light strikes an object.

Hypothesis B

Some of the light was diffracted by small particles on the surface of the mirror. The reflected light is not quite as bright because the diffracted part of the light bent around the edge of the mirror and continued in a different direction.

*Experiment 2*

In a second experiment, the students shined the light on a piece of aluminum foil that had been crumpled and then flattened. This time, they recorded the angle of reflection from a number of points. Figure 2 demonstrates how the light reflected from the material at each point.

Figure 2

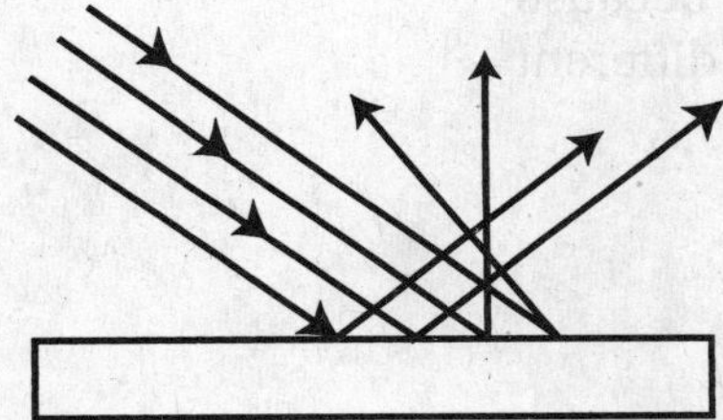

**31.** In Experiment 1, the mirror has a perfectly flat surface. If the angle labeled A on the diagram measures 46°, what is the measure of angle B?

**A.** 44°

**B.** 45°

**C.** 46°

**D.** 134°

**32.** Experiment 1 was repeated while the students measured the temperature of the mirror using a very sensitive thermometer. During the experiment, the temperature of the mirror increased by a small amount. How does this observation relate to the hypotheses concerning the loss of light intensity?

**F.** The observation supports hypothesis A because the light that was absorbed was converted into thermal energy.

**G.** The observation supports hypothesis B because diffracted photons transfer energy to the mirror by friction when they pass around the mirror's edge.

**H.** The observation supports both hypotheses because light is converted into thermal energy by both processes.

**J.** The observation does not support either hypothesis because heat and light are two different forms of energy.

**33.** While setting up Experiment 1, a student looked in the mirror at the reflection of the support used to hold the laser in place. Which statement best describes where the image appeared to be located?

**A.** The image appeared to be at the location of the object.

**B.** The image appeared to be on the surface of the mirror.

**C.** The image appeared to be a distance behind the mirror equal to the distance between the object and the mirror.

**D.** The image appeared to be in front of the mirror, close to the student's location.

**34.** Why did the reflections in Experiment 2 differ from the reflections in Experiment 1?

**F.** Light reflects differently from a metal, such as aluminum, than it does from a mirror.

**G.** Because the surface of the aluminum foil is uneven, parallel rays of light do not strike the surface at the same angle, so they do not reflect at the same angle.

**H.** The rays leave the aluminum foil at different angles because they reflect several times before they leave the foil's surface.

**J.** The aluminum foil and the mirror refract light differently, and the refraction changes the angle of reflection.

**35.** Which of these materials is likely to have a reflection pattern similar to the one shown in Figure 2?

**A.** A glass windowpane

**B.** A calm lake

**C.** A rough ocean

**D.** A polished stainless steel pan

Name Date

# Practice Test 4 *continued*

**Passage VII**

In the course of a roller coaster ride, energy changes form many times. A conveyor belt at the beginning of the ride is the only source of energy input. All of the energy required for the whole ride comes from work done by the conveyor belt as it lifts the cars and the passengers up the first hill. Figure 1 shows the first part of a roller coaster ride after the work of the conveyor belt has been completed.

Figure 1

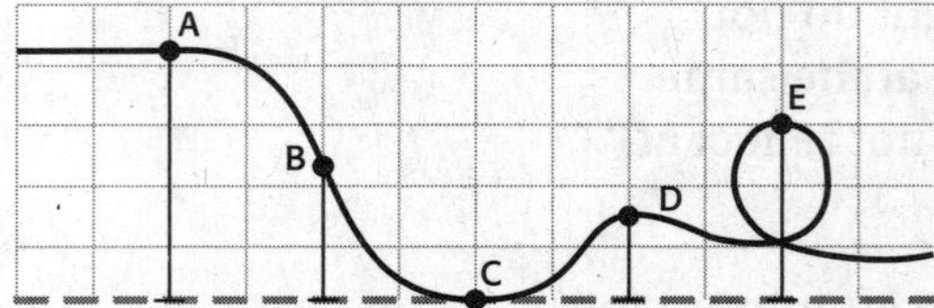


An engineer determined the kinetic energy of a roller coaster car at a number of points during the ride. The potential energy was calculated using the changes in kinetic energy during the ride. The energy information is plotted in Figure 2.

Figure 2

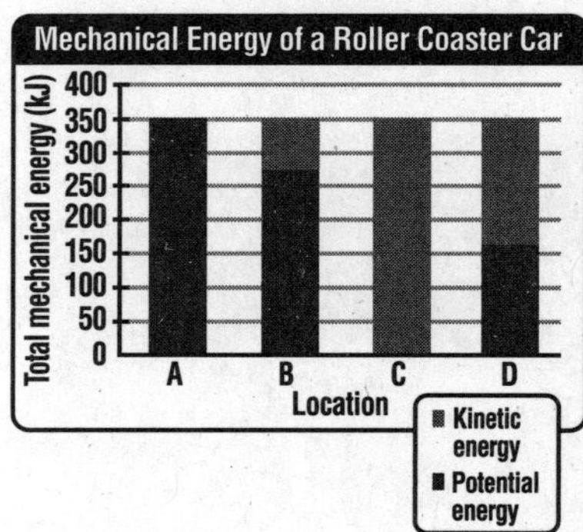

**36.** Based on Figures 1 and 2, what is the best estimate of the potential energy of the car at point E?

**F.** 75 kJ

**G.** 250 kJ

**H.** 300 kJ

**J.** 400 kJ

**37.** Based on Figures 1 and 2, the car moves slowest at which point on the ride?

**A.** Point A

**B.** Point C

**C.** Point D

**D.** Point E

**38.** Which statement below is the best analysis of the data presented in Figure 2?

**F.** The analysis accounts for all the energy transfers because energy is neither created nor destroyed, so the sum of the potential energy and kinetic energy of the car is constant.

**G.** The analysis is incomplete because it does not include the energy that is added by the application of the force of gravity as the car moves downward from Point A.

**H.** The analysis supports the fact that energy is neither created nor destroyed, but it does not account for energy that is transferred to the track as heat due to friction.

**J.** The analysis is incomplete because it does not include the energy that is added by the application of the upward force when the car begins to climb at Point C.

## Practice Test 4 *continued*

**39.** What energy transfer occurs between Point C and Point D of the roller coaster's motion on the track?

**A.** Mechanical energy is converted into kinetic energy as a conveyor belt pulls the car upward.

**B.** Kinetic energy is converted into potential energy as the force of gravity slows the car.

**C.** Kinetic energy is converted into mechanical energy as friction slows the car.

**D.** Potential energy is converted into kinetic energy as the force of gravity accelerates the car.

**40.** What factors affect the potential energy of the car at Point A in Figure 1?

**F.** The force of gravity on the car and the car's position relative to Earth's surface

**G.** The velocity of the car as it approaches the first drop

**H.** The speed with which the conveyor belt lifted the car

**J.** The friction of the wheels against the track and the air resistance on the moving car

# ACT Practice Test 5

Name Date

# Practice Test 5

## Passage I

A geologist drew the following cross-section of a hillside. At the bottom of the slope, an artesian spring feeds a stream that flows into a nearby river.

Figure 1

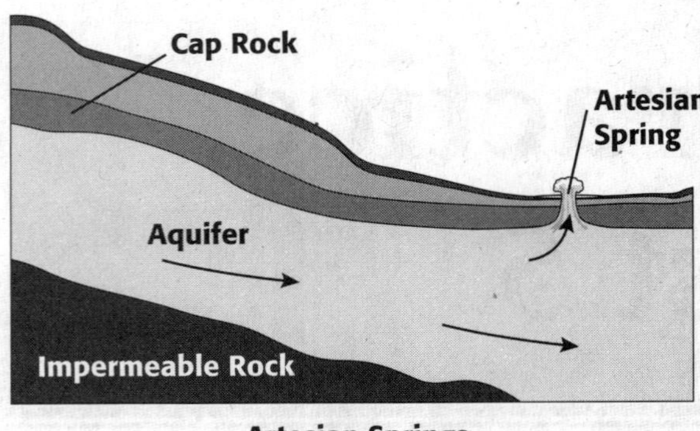


**Artesian Springs**

A test well was drilled on the slope through the cap rock and the rock of the aquifer and into the impermeable rock below. The top of the well was located at an elevation of 250 meters above sea level. The elevation of the artesian spring is 150 meters above sea level. The depth to the water table was measured each month for a year, and the data were recorded in Table 1. The amount of rainfall was also measured each month during the year, and the data were recorded in Table 2.

Table 1

| Depth of Well to Top of Water Table | |
|---|---|
| Month | Depth (m) |
| January | 75 |
| February | 85 |
| March | 70 |
| April | 50 |
| May | 75 |
| June | 90 |
| July | 125 |
| August | 150 |
| September | 75 |
| October | 60 |
| November | 60 |
| December | 50 |

Table 2

| Rainfall by Month | |
|---|---|
| Month | Rainfall (in.) |
| January | 2.3 |
| February | 4.5 |
| March | 2.8 |
| April | 3.5 |
| May | 0.4 |
| June | 0.5 |
| July | 5.1 |
| August | 4.2 |
| September | 3.8 |
| October | 4.0 |
| November | 3.9 |
| December | 3.3 |

# Practice Test 5 *continued*

**1.** What causes water to flow out of the ground at the artesian spring in Figure 1?

**A.** Pressure from the water that is above the level of the spring

**B.** The weight of the cap rock and other material above the aquifer

**C.** The upward push of the impermeable rock below the aquifer

**D.** Pressure from carbon dioxide and other gases trapped in the underground water of the aquifer

**2.** Which of the following statements correctly describes the location of an artesian spring?

**F.** Artesian springs are always located at the bottom of a slope or hillside.

**G.** An artesian spring develops at any place in which there is a crack or gap in the cap rock.

**H.** Artesian springs can develop at any elevation below the top of the water table if there is a break in the cap rock.

**J.** Artesian springs can develop at any place where an aquifer exists.

**3.** What materials make up the aquifer shown in Figure 1?

**A.** A large river of water flowing through cave-like openings below the surface of the ground

**B.** Water filling gaps and flowing through the cracks within nonporous rock layers

**C.** Alternating layers of rock and water under high pressure from the layers above

**D.** A layer of porous rock and stone with water filling the open space between rock particles

**4.** According to Table 1, during which months did water flow from the artesian spring at the bottom of the slope?

**F.** Every month of the year

**G.** Only during July and August

**H.** Every month except July and August

**J.** Every month except February, June, July, and August

# Practice Test 5 *continued*

**5.** Which of the following statements is the best description of how water reaches the aquifer based on the data shown in Tables 1 and 2?

**A.** The aquifer is replenished immediately as rain falls on the surface and passes through the cap rock.

**B.** The aquifer is replenished as water filters through the cap rock over a period of several days.

**C.** The aquifer is replenished by water that falls at elevations above the area shown in the diagram and then flows to the artesian spring in less than one month.

**D.** The aquifer is replenished by water that falls at elevations above the area shown in the diagram and then flows to the aquifer in about two months.

**6.** Based on Tables 1 and 2, how is the amount of water in the aquifer related to the amount of rainfall?

**F.** The aquifer contains a constant amount of water no matter how much rain falls.

**G.** The amount of water in the aquifer fluctuates in proportion to the rainfall over the previous several days.

**H.** The amount of water in the aquifer fluctuates roughly in proportion to the amount of rain, but with a two month delay.

**J.** The amount of water in the aquifer depends on the flow from the spring, not on the amount of rainfall.

**7.** Which statement best describes the recharge zone of an aquifer?

**A.** Anyplace that the water table of the aquifer meets the surface

**B.** The boundary between the aquifer and the permeable rock above it

**C.** An area above an aquifer that has significant amounts of rain or snow

**D.** A region from which surface water can travel through permeable rock to an aquifer

**Passage II**

A group of students conducted an experiment to measure the effect of color on the absorption of light energy when an object is placed in sunlight. They painted four cans, placed 500 grams of water in each can, and measured the temperature of the water as shown in Figure 1.

Figure 1

*Experiment 1*

The students placed the cans on a sunny windowsill for two hours. The students then measured the temperature again. The results are shown in Figure 2.

Figure 2

*Experiment 2*

After the second set of temperatures was recorded in Experiment 1, the four cans were placed on a shelf in the laboratory that received very little light. The temperature of the water in each can was measured after 2 hours. The temperature of each of the four cans was 21°C. When the temperatures were measured again the next morning, the water in each can was still 21°C.

# Practice Test 5 *continued*

**8.** In Experiment 1, what is the main cause for the increase in temperature of the water?

**F.** The cans absorbed the sunlight and transferred the energy to the water as heat.

**G.** The cans absorbed energy as a result of the collisions of particles in the air with the can and transferred the energy to the water as heat.

**H.** Sunlight warmed the ledge of the windowsill, which radiated the energy to the water.

**J.** The water inside the cans absorbed the energy of sunlight and converted it into thermal energy.

**9.** For Experiment 1, which statement correctly describes the significance of the temperature changes shown?

**A.** The water molecules in the white can slowed down more than the water molecules in any other can did.

**B.** The water molecules in the black can had a larger increase in average kinetic energy than the water molecules in any other can had.

**C.** The water molecules in the blue can have a lower average potential energy than the water molecules in the white can have.

**D.** The water molecules in the yellow can are moving at half the speed of the water molecules in the blue can.

**10.** In Experiment 2, why did the cans of water all come to the same temperature over a period of time when they were removed from the sunlight?

**F.** Energy as heat was transferred from the surrounding air to the cans until the cans were at the same temperature.

**G.** Energy as heat was transferred from the water to the cooler air until both were at the same temperature.

**H.** Heat was transferred between adjacent cans until they reached the same temperature.

**J.** Some water absorbed energy and evaporated from the cans, which cooled the remaining water.

# Practice Test 5 *continued*

**11.** Why did the cans not all warm to the same temperature in Experiment 1?

**A.** The final temperature depends on the total mass of water in the can.

**B.** Darker colored cans are better insulators than lighter colored cans are.

**C.** The light colored cans were most likely placed in a shady spot while the dark colored cans were placed in a sunny spot.

**D.** The darker colored cans absorbed more wavelengths of light than the lighter colored cans did, so the darker colored cans gained more energy.

**12.** Which of the following statements correctly describes the results of Experiment 1?

**F.** More energy was created in the black can and less energy was created in the white can.

**G.** No energy was created or destroyed during the experiment, but some energy changed form.

**H.** The results of this experiment involved only temperature changes because no energy changes were directly observed.

**J.** The observation that cans in a single environment reached different temperatures is evidence that the law of conservation of energy does not apply in all cases.

**13.** Based on the results of Experiment 2, what was the temperature of the air around the cans the next morning?

**A.** The temperature was 21°C because no net energy transfer was occurring between the cans and the air.

**B.** The temperature was less than 21°C because water has a greater specific heat than air has.

**C.** The temperature was greater than 21°C because water has a greater specific heat than air has.

**D.** The temperature was 20°C because the water will continue to cool down until it returns to its original temperature.

# Practice Test 5 *continued*

## Passage III

A Punnett square is a diagram that is used to predict the possible outcomes of a particular breeding event. It is a summary of the possible combinations of alleles of a particular gene based on the genetic makeup of the parents. Biologists use the Punnett square to predict the probability that offspring will have a particular genotype, or combination of alleles. The square also helps to predict the phenotype, or appearance, of each possible offspring based on the traits associated with the dominant and recessive alleles.

For example, the Punnett square in Figure 1 shows the possible combinations of alleles for a cross between two pea plants. One parent has two alleles for tall growth (*T*), and the second parent has an allele for tall growth and an allele for short growth (*t*). The allele for tall growth uses an uppercase letter *T* to show that it is the dominant allele.

Figure 1

| *TT* × *Tt* | *T* | *t* |
|---|---|---|
| *T* | *TT* | *Tt* |
| *T* | *TT* | *Tt* |

The organisms in Figure 1 that have the genotype *TT* are called *homozygous* because both alleles of this particular gene are the same. The organisms in Figure 1 that have the genotype *Tt* are called *heterozygous* because the two alleles are different.

Figure 2 shows a cross between two rabbits. Black fur (*B*) is dominant to brown fur (*b*).

Figure 2

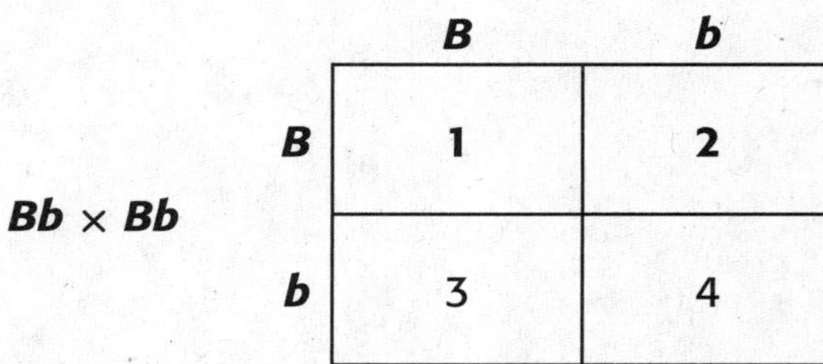


A breeder kept records of the colors of the rabbits born to various pairs of parents. Figures 3 and 4 show the results for two litters of five bunnies that were bred from two different pairs of black rabbits.

Name Date

# Practice Test 5 *continued*

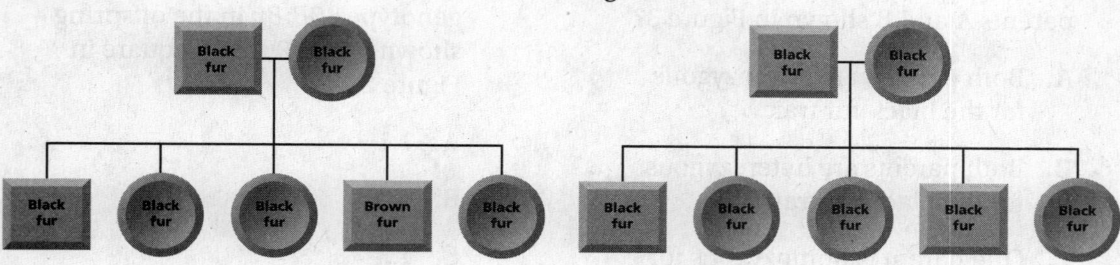


**14.** What is the ratio of tall to short phenotypes for the offspring shown in the Punnett square in Figure 1?

**F.** 1:3

**G.** 2:2

**H.** 3:1

**J.** 4:0

**15.** If the offspring shown in Figure 1 are crossed randomly in the next generation, what genotypes could be produced?

**A.** *TT* and *tt* only

**B.** *tt* only

**C.** *Tt* only

**D.** *TT, tt,* and *Tt*

**16.** What are the possible genotypes for a cross between two pea plants with genotypes *TT* and *tt*?

**F.** *TT* only

**G.** *tt* only

**H.** *Tt* only

**J.** *TT, tt,* and *Tt*

# Practice Test 5 *continued*

**17.** Which statement below is true of parents A and B shown in Figure 3?

**A.** Both parents are homozygous for the black-fur trait.

**B.** Both parents are heterozygous for the black-fur trait.

**C.** One parent is homozygous for fur color and the other parent is heterozygous for fur color.

**D.** The bunny with brown fur is a mutant because its fur color would be predicted to be black.

**18.** Which statement below is true of parents C and D shown in Figure 4?

**F.** Both parents must be homozygous for the black fur trait.

**G.** At least one parent must be heterozygous for the black fur trait

**H.** Both parents must be either homozygous or heterozygous for the black fur trait.

**J.** At least one parent must be homozygous for the black fur trait.

**19.** What would be the ratio of genotypes *BB*:*Bb* in the offspring shown in the Punnett square in Figure 2?

**A.** 1:1

**B.** 1:2

**C.** 1:3

**D.** 3:1

# Practice Test 5 *continued*

**Passage IV**

A chemical equation uses symbols and formulas to represent the identities and relative molecular or molar amounts of the reactants and products in a chemical reaction. Chemical equations are very useful in doing quantitative chemical work. The arrow in a balanced chemical equation is like an equals sign. And the chemical equation as a whole is similar to an algebraic equation in that it expresses an equality. For example, the following chemical equation shows that the reactant ammonium dichromate yields the products nitrogen, chromium(III) oxide, and water.

$$(NH_4)_2Cr_2O_7(s) \rightarrow N_2(g) + Cr_2O_3(s) + 4H_2O(g)$$

This equation indicates that 1 mole of ammonium dichromate reacts to form 1 mole of nitrogen, one mole of chromium (III) oxide, and 4 moles of water. According to the law of conservation of mass, matter is neither created nor destroyed during a chemical reaction. In addition, atoms of a particular element do not change into atoms of a different element during a chemical reaction, so the number of atoms of each element must be the same before and after the reaction. Coefficients are used to balance the equation and keep the number of atoms of each element the same on both sides of the equation.

The coefficients show the relative number of moles of each reactant used and each product formed, not an absolute number. A reactant that is completely used up in a reaction limits the amount of the other reactant that is used and also limits the amount of product that can form in a chemical reaction, so it is called the *limiting reactant.* A limiting reactant may also be referred to as a limiting reagent. The substance that is not used up completely in a reaction is called the *excess reactant.* The number of moles of product that can form can be determined using the balanced chemical equation and the number of moles of each reactant that are available.

The relative mass of each reactant and each product shown in an equation can be calculated by multiplying the number of moles of a substance by its molar mass, which is the mass in grams of one mole of the substance.

*Experiment 1*
In a laboratory experiment, a chemist combined sodium sulfate with calcium carbonate and carbon to form sodium carbonate, carbon dioxide, and calcium sulfide. The chemical equation for the reaction is:

$$Na_2SO_4 + CaCO_3 + 2C \rightarrow Na_2CO_3(s) + 2CO_2 + CaS$$

# Practice Test 5 *continued*

**The chemist prepared Tables 1 and 2 for the materials used in the reaction.**

Table 1

| Reactants | Mass (g) | Molar mass (g/mol) | Amount (mol) |
|---|---|---|---|
| sodium sulfate | 500. | 142.1 | 3.52 |
| calcium carbonate | 800. | 100.1 | 7.99 |
| Carbon | 24.0 | 12.0 | 2.00 |

Table 2

| Products | Mass (g) | Molar mass (g/mol) | Amount (mol) |
|---|---|---|---|
| sodium carbonate | | 106.0 | |
| carbon dioxide | | 44.0 | |
| calcium sulfide | | 72.1 | |

*Experiment 2*

**During a different experiment, the scientist studied the combustion of methane according to the equation below.**

$CH_4(g) + 2O_2(g) \rightarrow CO_2(g) + 2H_2O$

*Experiment 3*

**A third experiment was performed in which magnesium metal was burned in oxygen to produce magnesium oxide according to the equation below.**

$2Mg(s) + O_2(g) \rightarrow 2MgO(s)$

**To help an assistant perform the necessary calculations, the chemist gathered together the molar masses of the elements that compose the substances involved in the reactions in Experiments 2 and 3 and recorded them in Table 3.**

Table 3

| Element | Molar mass (g/mol) |
|---|---|
| carbon | 12.0 |
| hydrogen | 1.0 |
| oxygen | 16.0 |
| magnesium | 24.3 |

# Practice Test 5 *continued*

**20.** In Experiment 1, how many moles of calcium sulfide will be formed during the reaction?

**F.** 1.00 mol

**G.** 2.00 mol

**H.** 4.00 mol

**J.** 7.99 mol

**21.** In Experiment 1, what mass of carbon dioxide will be formed during the reaction

**A.** 22.0 g

**B.** 44.0 g

**C.** 88.0 g

**D.** 176.0 g

**22.** In Experiment 1, when 4.00 moles of each reactant are combined and the reaction is allowed to go to completion, what mass of sodium carbonate would be expected to be produced?

**F.** 106 g

**G.** 212 g

**H.** 424 g

**J.** 848 g

**23.** In Experiment 2, what mass of water should be produced during the combustion of 2.00 moles of methane?

**A.** 18.0 g

**B.** 29.0 g

**C.** 36.0 g

**D.** 72.0 g

**24.** What mass of magnesium oxide forms in Experiment 3 when 2.00 moles of magnesium burns?

**F.** 40.3 g

**G.** 48.6 g

**H.** 56.3 g

**J.** 80.6 g

**25.** The chemist plans for another experiment to study the combustion of butane, $C_4H_{10}$. In the reaction below, which coefficients will balance the equation?

$C_4H_{10} + O_2 \rightarrow CO_2 + H_2O$

**A.** 1, 4, 4, 5

**B.** 2, 13, 8, 10

**C.** 1, 4, 6, 5

**D.** 2, 5, 8, 5

**Passage V**

Wegener's Theory of Continental Drift was not immediately accepted because there was no known mechanism for the motion of the continents. A series of discoveries on the sea floor led to a new theory–plate tectonics–based on the idea of continents floating on the mantle beneath them. Sea-floor spreading formed the basis of the new theory. Key observations in developing the concept of sea-floor spreading were:

*Observation 1*
Sediment that covers the floor of the ocean is thinnest at the mid-ocean ridges and grows increasingly thicker with distance from the ridge.

*Observation 2*
Ocean crust near mid-ocean ridges is relatively young and grows increasingly older with distance from the ridge.

*Observation 3*
Magnetic particles in rock form "stripes" that are parallel to the mid-ocean ridge. These stripes show alternating patterns of magnetic polarity.

*Observation 4*
The patterns of magnetic stripes are symmetrical across the mid-ocean ridges, with the pattern on one side forming a mirror image of the pattern on the other side.

**Figure 1: Mid-Ocean Ridge**

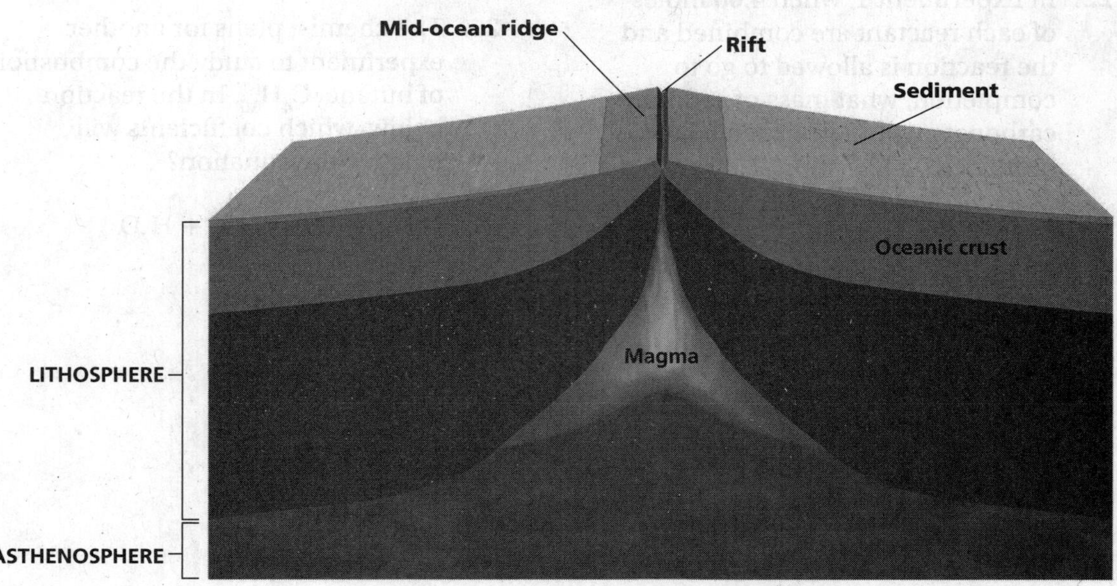

# Practice Test 5 *continued*

**Table 1: PLATE BOUNDARY SUMMARY**

| Type of boundary | Description | Example |
|---|---|---|
| Divergent ← → | plates moving away from each other to form rifts and mid-ocean ridges | North American and Eurasian plates at the Mid-Atlantic Ridge |
| Convergent → ← | plates moving toward each other and colliding to form ocean trenches, mountain ranges, volcanoes, and island arcs | South American and Nazca plates at the Chilean trench along the west coast of South America |
| Transform ⇆ | plates sliding past each other while moving in opposite directions | North Americann and Pacific plates at the San Andreas Fault in California |

**26.** Which statement correctly uses Observations 1 and 2 to support the concept of sea-floor spreading?

**F.** New rock forms at the mid-ocean ridge and scrapes sediment off of older rock as it ages and moves away from the ridge.

**G.** As it ages, rock on the ocean floor moves away from the mid-ocean ridge and, over time, sediment is deposited on it and increases in depth with distance from the ridge.

**H.** New rock forms as material ejected from the mid-ocean ridge is carried by currents away from the ridge and spreads out to cover the ocean floor.

**J.** As it ages, rock on the ocean floor moves toward the mid-ocean ridge and gradually loses its overburden of sediment.

**27.** Which of the following statements strengthens the support for sea-floor spreading that is provided by Observations 3 and 4?

**A.** There are active volcanoes at a mid-ocean ridge.

**B.** At the mid-ocean ridge, two plates slide past one another.

**C.** Magnetic particles in a rock align long after the rock has been formed.

**D.** Rocks on land show that Earth's magnetic field periodically reverses direction.

# Practice Test 5 *continued*

**28.** Off the west coast of South America, one tectonic plate is sinking beneath another plate. Based on Figure 2, what feature would you expect to find here?

**F.** A mid-ocean ridge

**G.** A trench

**H.** An abyssal plain

**J.** A rift

**29.** The ocean floor moves away from the mid-ocean ridge after it is formed. As the lithosphere ages, which of the following occurs?

**A.** The ocean floor's density decreases, making it more volcanic.

**B.** The ocean floor is immediately returned to the asthenosphere where it melts again.

**C.** The ocean floor's temperature increases and its density decreases until it melts back into magma.

**D.** The ocean floor sinks as its temperature decreases and its density increases.

**30.** The island of Iceland is located at the boundary of the North American and Eurasian plates. Existing cracks in the ground have been observed to be slowly widening over a long period of time. Based on Figure 2, what explanation can be given for these features?

**F.** Iceland is located near a mid-ocean trench where two plates are colliding

**G.** Iceland forms a small section of very old continental crust surrounded by oceanic crust.

**H.** Iceland is located along the divergent plate boundary that forms the mid-ocean ridge in the Atlantic Ocean.

**J.** The plates on which Europe and North America are located are moving past one another and are opening the crust near Iceland.

# Practice Test 5 *continued*

## Passage VI

*Experiment 1*

In a laboratory, a scientist applied pushes and pulls to a 1 kg block using devices that measured the applied force. The forces were applied in four directions as shown in Figure 1. Sensors recorded the motion of the block each second for 4 sec, as shown in Table 1, and a computer calculated the average velocity for each 1-sec period.

Figure 1

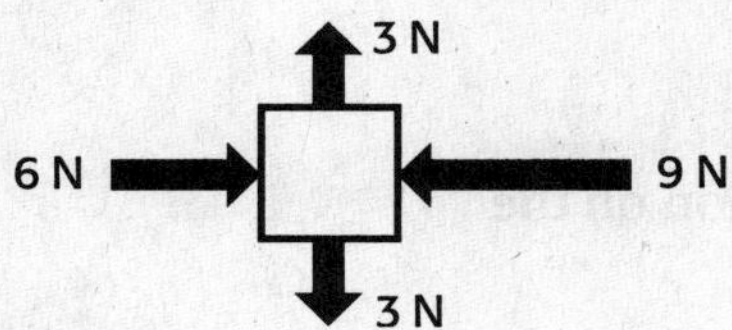


Table 1

| Motion of Block | | |
|---|---|---|
| Time (sec) | Position (m) | Velocity (m/sec) |
| 0.0 | 0.0 | 0.0 |
| 1.0 | 1.0 | 2.0 |
| 2.0 | 4.0 | 4.0 |
| 3.0 | 9.0 | 6.0 |
| 4.0 | 16.0 | 8.0 |

*Experiment 2*

For this experiment, the scientist placed the same block used in Experiment 1 on a rough surface. The force of friction between the block and the surface was measured as 3 N.

*Experiment 3*

In a separate experiment, a force was applied in one direction to a block of unknown mass. The block and surface were treated with a lubricant so that friction was reduced to a level that was not measurable. Force was applied, and the acceleration was measured and recorded in Table 2.

Table 2

| Trial | Acceleration | Applied force |
|---|---|---|
| 1 | 0.70 $m/s^2$ | 0.35 N |
| 2 | 1.70 $m/s^2$ | 0.85 N |
| 3 | 2.70 $m/s^2$ | 1.35 N |
| 4 | 3.70 $m/s^2$ | 1.85 N |
| 5 | 4.70 $m/s^2$ | 2.35 N |

**31.** According to the data in Table 1, what was the acceleration of the block during the experiment?

**A.** 0.5 m/sec$^2$

**B.** 1.0 m/sec$^2$

**C.** 2.0 m/sec$^2$

**D.** 4.0 m/sec$^2$

**32.** What was the force of friction on the block in Experiment 1?

**F.** 1.0 N to the right

**G.** 1.0 N to the left

**H.** 2.0 N to the left

**J.** 3.0 N to the right

**33.** What was the acceleration of the 1 kg block during Experiment 2?

**A.** 0.0 m/sec$^2$

**B.** 2.0 m/sec$^2$ to the right

**C.** 4.0 m/sec$^2$ to the right

**D.** 16.0 m/sec$^2$ to the right

**34.** What is the mass of the block used to collect the data in Table 2?

**F.** 0.25 kg

**G.** 0.5 kg

**H.** 2.0 kg

**J.** 5.0 kg

**35.** In trial 3 of Experiment 3, what is the speed of the block after the force is applied for 4 sec if the block started from rest?

**A.** 0.675 m/sec

**B.** 10.8 m/sec

**C.** 14.8 m/sec

**D.** 18.8 m/sec

# Practice Test 5 *continued*

## Passage VII

The elements of the periodic table are classified into groups, or families, based on their properties. The elements in a family have the same number of valence electrons and form a column on the table.

**Figure 1 Classification of the Elements**

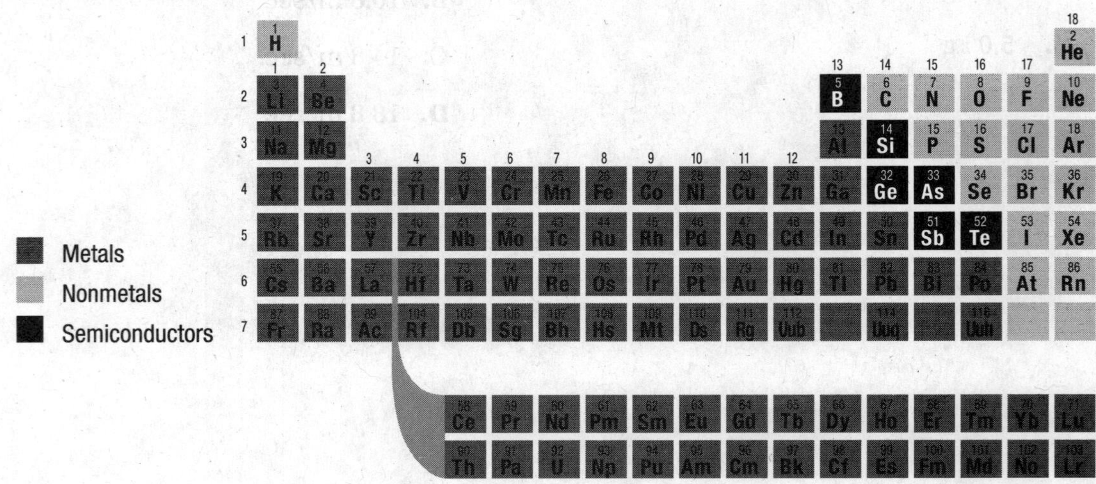


**Table 1 Element Families**

| Group number | Number of valence electrons | Name of family |
|---|---|---|
| Group 1 | 1 | alkali metals |
| Group 2 | 2 | alkaline-earth metals |
| Groups 3–12 | varied | transition metals |
| Group 17 | 7 | halogens |
| Group 18 | 8* | noble gases |

**except helium, which has two electrons*

Ionic compounds form when atoms (or in some cases, groups of atoms) gain or lose electrons to form ions. Ions with opposite charges are attracted to one another by electric forces and form compounds. Metal atoms tend to form ions by losing their valence electrons and achieving an electron configuration that matches the electron configuration of the noble gas that falls before the metal on the periodic table. As a result, these ions have one or more excess positive charges. Nonmetal atoms tend to gain electrons until they have an electron configuration that matches the electron configuration of the noble gas that falls after the nonmetal on the periodic table. As a result, these ions have one or more excess negative charges. Ions that join to form a compound must have a net charge of zero.

# Practice Test 5 *continued*

**36.** Based on the information in Figure 1 and in Table 1, predict the formula of the ionic compound magnesium iodide.

**F.** MgI

**G.** $Mg_2I$

**H.** $MgI_2$

**J.** $Mg_2I_3$

**37.** Based on the information in Figure 1 and in Table 1, which family of elements includes iron?

**A.** Alkali metals

**B.** Alkaline earth metals

**C.** Transition metals

**D.** Halogens

**38.** A scientist examines the properties of an unknown element, X, and finds that it forms the following ionic compounds: $Li_2X$, MgX, $Al_2X_3$. In what group of the periodic table is element X located?

**F.** 14

**G.** 15

**H.** 16

**J.** 17

# Practice Test 5 *continued*

**39.** When Mendeleev made his periodic table, he did not include any noble gases because none of them had been discovered at that time. Which of the following statements is a reasonable explanation for why no group 18 elements were known at that time?

**A.** The elements in group 18 are all gases, so none of them could be detected in the middle of the 19th century.

**B.** The elements in group 18 were not detected because they have full electron shells and therefore do not react with other elements.

**C.** The noble gases were not known at that time because they are so rare that very sensitive instruments are needed in order to detect them

**D.** The group 18 elements do not occur naturally on Earth so they were not detected in the 19th century.

**40.** Based on the information in Figure 1 and in Table 1, predict the formula of the ionic compound sodium oxide.

**F.** NaO

**G.** $Na_2O$

**H.** $NaO_2$

**J.** $So_2O$

Name ______________________________ Date ______________

# Practice Test 1 Answer Sheet

1 (A) (B) (C) (D)
2 (F) (G) (H) (J)
3 (A) (B) (C) (D)
4 (F) (G) (H) (J)
5 (A) (B) (C) (D)
6 (F) (G) (H) (J)
7 (A) (B) (C) (D)
8 (F) (G) (H) (J)
9 (A) (B) (C) (D)
10 (F) (G) (H) (J)
11 (A) (B) (C) (D)
12 (F) (G) (H) (J)
13 (A) (B) (C) (D)
14 (F) (G) (H) (J)
15 (A) (B) (C) (D)
16 (F) (G) (H) (J)
17 (A) (B) (C) (D)
18 (F) (G) (H) (J)
19 (A) (B) (C) (D)
20 (F) (G) (H) (J)
21 (A) (B) (C) (D)
22 (F) (G) (H) (J)
23 (A) (B) (C) (D)
24 (F) (G) (H) (J)
25 (A) (B) (C) (D)
26 (F) (G) (H) (J)
27 (A) (B) (C) (D)
28 (F) (G) (H) (J)
29 (A) (B) (C) (D)
30 (F) (G) (H) (J)
31 (A) (B) (C) (D)
32 (F) (G) (H) (J)
33 (A) (B) (C) (D)
34 (F) (G) (H) (J)
35 (A) (B) (C) (D)
36 (F) (G) (H) (J)
37 (A) (B) (C) (D)
38 (F) (G) (H) (J)
39 (A) (B) (C) (D)
40 (F) (G) (H) (J)

Name ______________________________ Date ______________

# Practice Test 2 Answer Sheet

| | | | | | | | | | |
|---|---|---|---|---|---|---|---|---|---|
| 1 | Ⓐ | Ⓑ | Ⓒ | Ⓓ | 21 | Ⓐ | Ⓑ | Ⓒ | Ⓓ |
| 2 | Ⓕ | Ⓖ | Ⓗ | Ⓙ | 22 | Ⓕ | Ⓖ | Ⓗ | Ⓙ |
| 3 | Ⓐ | Ⓑ | Ⓒ | Ⓓ | 23 | Ⓐ | Ⓑ | Ⓒ | Ⓓ |
| 4 | Ⓕ | Ⓖ | Ⓗ | Ⓙ | 24 | Ⓕ | Ⓖ | Ⓗ | Ⓙ |
| 5 | Ⓐ | Ⓑ | Ⓒ | Ⓓ | 25 | Ⓐ | Ⓑ | Ⓒ | Ⓓ |
| 6 | Ⓕ | Ⓖ | Ⓗ | Ⓙ | 26 | Ⓕ | Ⓖ | Ⓗ | Ⓙ |
| 7 | Ⓐ | Ⓑ | Ⓒ | Ⓓ | 27 | Ⓐ | Ⓑ | Ⓒ | Ⓓ |
| 8 | Ⓕ | Ⓖ | Ⓗ | Ⓙ | 28 | Ⓕ | Ⓖ | Ⓗ | Ⓙ |
| 9 | Ⓐ | Ⓑ | Ⓒ | Ⓓ | 29 | Ⓐ | Ⓑ | Ⓒ | Ⓓ |
| 10 | Ⓕ | Ⓖ | Ⓗ | Ⓙ | 30 | Ⓕ | Ⓖ | Ⓗ | Ⓙ |
| 11 | Ⓐ | Ⓑ | Ⓒ | Ⓓ | 31 | Ⓐ | Ⓑ | Ⓒ | Ⓓ |
| 12 | Ⓕ | Ⓖ | Ⓗ | Ⓙ | 32 | Ⓕ | Ⓖ | Ⓗ | Ⓙ |
| 13 | Ⓐ | Ⓑ | Ⓒ | Ⓓ | 33 | Ⓐ | Ⓑ | Ⓒ | Ⓓ |
| 14 | Ⓕ | Ⓖ | Ⓗ | Ⓙ | 34 | Ⓕ | Ⓖ | Ⓗ | Ⓙ |
| 15 | Ⓐ | Ⓑ | Ⓒ | Ⓓ | 35 | Ⓐ | Ⓑ | Ⓒ | Ⓓ |
| 16 | Ⓕ | Ⓖ | Ⓗ | Ⓙ | 36 | Ⓕ | Ⓖ | Ⓗ | Ⓙ |
| 17 | Ⓐ | Ⓑ | Ⓒ | Ⓓ | 37 | Ⓐ | Ⓑ | Ⓒ | Ⓓ |
| 18 | Ⓕ | Ⓖ | Ⓗ | Ⓙ | 38 | Ⓕ | Ⓖ | Ⓗ | Ⓙ |
| 19 | Ⓐ | Ⓑ | Ⓒ | Ⓓ | 39 | Ⓐ | Ⓑ | Ⓒ | Ⓓ |
| 20 | Ⓕ | Ⓖ | Ⓗ | Ⓙ | 40 | Ⓕ | Ⓖ | Ⓗ | Ⓙ |

Name ______________________________ Date ______________

# Practice Test 3 Answer Sheet

| | | | | | | | | | |
|---|---|---|---|---|---|---|---|---|---|
| 1 | Ⓐ | Ⓑ | Ⓒ | Ⓓ | 21 | Ⓐ | Ⓑ | Ⓒ | Ⓓ |
| 2 | Ⓕ | Ⓖ | Ⓗ | Ⓙ | 22 | Ⓕ | Ⓖ | Ⓗ | Ⓙ |
| 3 | Ⓐ | Ⓑ | Ⓒ | Ⓓ | 23 | Ⓐ | Ⓑ | Ⓒ | Ⓓ |
| 4 | Ⓕ | Ⓖ | Ⓗ | Ⓙ | 24 | Ⓕ | Ⓖ | Ⓗ | Ⓙ |
| 5 | Ⓐ | Ⓑ | Ⓒ | Ⓓ | 25 | Ⓐ | Ⓑ | Ⓒ | Ⓓ |
| 6 | Ⓕ | Ⓖ | Ⓗ | Ⓙ | 26 | Ⓕ | Ⓖ | Ⓗ | Ⓙ |
| 7 | Ⓐ | Ⓑ | Ⓒ | Ⓓ | 27 | Ⓐ | Ⓑ | Ⓒ | Ⓓ |
| 8 | Ⓕ | Ⓖ | Ⓗ | Ⓙ | 28 | Ⓕ | Ⓖ | Ⓗ | Ⓙ |
| 9 | Ⓐ | Ⓑ | Ⓒ | Ⓓ | 29 | Ⓐ | Ⓑ | Ⓒ | Ⓓ |
| 10 | Ⓕ | Ⓖ | Ⓗ | Ⓙ | 30 | Ⓕ | Ⓖ | Ⓗ | Ⓙ |
| 11 | Ⓐ | Ⓑ | Ⓒ | Ⓓ | 31 | Ⓐ | Ⓑ | Ⓒ | Ⓓ |
| 12 | Ⓕ | Ⓖ | Ⓗ | Ⓙ | 32 | Ⓕ | Ⓖ | Ⓗ | Ⓙ |
| 13 | Ⓐ | Ⓑ | Ⓒ | Ⓓ | 33 | Ⓐ | Ⓑ | Ⓒ | Ⓓ |
| 14 | Ⓕ | Ⓖ | Ⓗ | Ⓙ | 34 | Ⓕ | Ⓖ | Ⓗ | Ⓙ |
| 15 | Ⓐ | Ⓑ | Ⓒ | Ⓓ | 35 | Ⓐ | Ⓑ | Ⓒ | Ⓓ |
| 16 | Ⓕ | Ⓖ | Ⓗ | Ⓙ | 36 | Ⓕ | Ⓖ | Ⓗ | Ⓙ |
| 17 | Ⓐ | Ⓑ | Ⓒ | Ⓓ | 37 | Ⓐ | Ⓑ | Ⓒ | Ⓓ |
| 18 | Ⓕ | Ⓖ | Ⓗ | Ⓙ | 38 | Ⓕ | Ⓖ | Ⓗ | Ⓙ |
| 19 | Ⓐ | Ⓑ | Ⓒ | Ⓓ | 39 | Ⓐ | Ⓑ | Ⓒ | Ⓓ |
| 20 | Ⓕ | Ⓖ | Ⓗ | Ⓙ | 40 | Ⓕ | Ⓖ | Ⓗ | Ⓙ |

Name ______________________ Date ____________

# Practice Test 4 Answer Sheet

1 Ⓐ Ⓑ Ⓒ Ⓓ
2 Ⓕ Ⓖ Ⓗ Ⓙ
3 Ⓐ Ⓑ Ⓒ Ⓓ
4 Ⓕ Ⓖ Ⓗ Ⓙ
5 Ⓐ Ⓑ Ⓒ Ⓓ
6 Ⓕ Ⓖ Ⓗ Ⓙ
7 Ⓐ Ⓑ Ⓒ Ⓓ
8 Ⓕ Ⓖ Ⓗ Ⓙ
9 Ⓐ Ⓑ Ⓒ Ⓓ
10 Ⓕ Ⓖ Ⓗ Ⓙ
11 Ⓐ Ⓑ Ⓒ Ⓓ
12 Ⓕ Ⓖ Ⓗ Ⓙ
13 Ⓐ Ⓑ Ⓒ Ⓓ
14 Ⓕ Ⓖ Ⓗ Ⓙ
15 Ⓐ Ⓑ Ⓒ Ⓓ
16 Ⓕ Ⓖ Ⓗ Ⓙ
17 Ⓐ Ⓑ Ⓒ Ⓓ
18 Ⓕ Ⓖ Ⓗ Ⓙ
19 Ⓐ Ⓑ Ⓒ Ⓓ
20 Ⓕ Ⓖ Ⓗ Ⓙ
21 Ⓐ Ⓑ Ⓒ Ⓓ
22 Ⓕ Ⓖ Ⓗ Ⓙ
23 Ⓐ Ⓑ Ⓒ Ⓓ
24 Ⓕ Ⓖ Ⓗ Ⓙ
25 Ⓐ Ⓑ Ⓒ Ⓓ
26 Ⓕ Ⓖ Ⓗ Ⓙ
27 Ⓐ Ⓑ Ⓒ Ⓓ
28 Ⓕ Ⓖ Ⓗ Ⓙ
29 Ⓐ Ⓑ Ⓒ Ⓓ
30 Ⓕ Ⓖ Ⓗ Ⓙ
31 Ⓐ Ⓑ Ⓒ Ⓓ
32 Ⓕ Ⓖ Ⓗ Ⓙ
33 Ⓐ Ⓑ Ⓒ Ⓓ
34 Ⓕ Ⓖ Ⓗ Ⓙ
35 Ⓐ Ⓑ Ⓒ Ⓓ
36 Ⓕ Ⓖ Ⓗ Ⓙ
37 Ⓐ Ⓑ Ⓒ Ⓓ
38 Ⓕ Ⓖ Ⓗ Ⓙ
39 Ⓐ Ⓑ Ⓒ Ⓓ
40 Ⓕ Ⓖ Ⓗ Ⓙ

Name ______________________________ Date ______________

# Practice Test 5 Answer Sheet

1 Ⓐ Ⓑ Ⓒ Ⓓ
2 Ⓕ Ⓖ Ⓗ Ⓙ
3 Ⓐ Ⓑ Ⓒ Ⓓ
4 Ⓕ Ⓖ Ⓗ Ⓙ
5 Ⓐ Ⓑ Ⓒ Ⓓ
6 Ⓕ Ⓖ Ⓗ Ⓙ
7 Ⓐ Ⓑ Ⓒ Ⓓ
8 Ⓕ Ⓖ Ⓗ Ⓙ
9 Ⓐ Ⓑ Ⓒ Ⓓ
10 Ⓕ Ⓖ Ⓗ Ⓙ
11 Ⓐ Ⓑ Ⓒ Ⓓ
12 Ⓕ Ⓖ Ⓗ Ⓙ
13 Ⓐ Ⓑ Ⓒ Ⓓ
14 Ⓕ Ⓖ Ⓗ Ⓙ
15 Ⓐ Ⓑ Ⓒ Ⓓ
16 Ⓕ Ⓖ Ⓗ Ⓙ
17 Ⓐ Ⓑ Ⓒ Ⓓ
18 Ⓕ Ⓖ Ⓗ Ⓙ
19 Ⓐ Ⓑ Ⓒ Ⓓ
20 Ⓕ Ⓖ Ⓗ Ⓙ
21 Ⓐ Ⓑ Ⓒ Ⓓ
22 Ⓕ Ⓖ Ⓗ Ⓙ
23 Ⓐ Ⓑ Ⓒ Ⓓ
24 Ⓕ Ⓖ Ⓗ Ⓙ
25 Ⓐ Ⓑ Ⓒ Ⓓ
26 Ⓕ Ⓖ Ⓗ Ⓙ
27 Ⓐ Ⓑ Ⓒ Ⓓ
28 Ⓕ Ⓖ Ⓗ Ⓙ
29 Ⓐ Ⓑ Ⓒ Ⓓ
30 Ⓕ Ⓖ Ⓗ Ⓙ
31 Ⓐ Ⓑ Ⓒ Ⓓ
32 Ⓕ Ⓖ Ⓗ Ⓙ
33 Ⓐ Ⓑ Ⓒ Ⓓ
34 Ⓕ Ⓖ Ⓗ Ⓙ
35 Ⓐ Ⓑ Ⓒ Ⓓ
36 Ⓕ Ⓖ Ⓗ Ⓙ
37 Ⓐ Ⓑ Ⓒ Ⓓ
38 Ⓕ Ⓖ Ⓗ Ⓙ
39 Ⓐ Ⓑ Ⓒ Ⓓ
40 Ⓕ Ⓖ Ⓗ Ⓙ